NARCISSISTIC MEN AND THE WOMEN WHO LOVE THEM

HOW TO BREAK FREE FROM ABUSE, FIND HEALING
FROM THE EFFECTS OF NARCISSISM AND
EMBRACE THE JOURNEY TO RECOVERY AND
FREEDOM

EVA JENSSEN

CONTENTS

Introduction   7

PART 1: WHAT IT IS
1. Who Is This Guy?   17
2. Why Me?   35

PART 2: HOW IT PLAYS OUT
3. The Pattern of a Narcissistic Relationship   51
4. The Idealization Stage   63
5. The Devaluation Stage   75
6. The Discard Stage   91

PART 3: HOW IT ENDS
7. The Beginning of the End   99
8. Who Am I?   113
9. Drawing the Line in the Sand   128
10. Deciding on the Fate of the Relationship   143
11. Planning a New Future   155

Afterword   165
References   171

QUICK GUIDE TO SPOTTING A NARCISSIST

(DON'T GET CAUGHT EASILY!)

jenssenbooks.com

Receive your FREE Quick Quiz Checklist to help you:

- Quickly evaluate whether your current partner is a Narcissist?
- Easily spot a Narcissist in the future and avoid getting caught in their trap!

To download your free Quick Quiz Checklist, click:

https://jenssenbooks.activehosted.com/f/1

INTRODUCTION

So, you met a guy.

He was full-on!

Loud, charismatic, charming. But full-on!

You know his type, you've seen it all before - a little self-absorbed, a little too confident, but the life of the party, nonetheless.

Everyone surrounds him. You roll your eyes, you know his game, but still, his flirty remarks, those sneaky little comments that make you feel seen amidst the crowd; they get under your skin and spark a little excitement. You're determined to show him that you know his type and keep the power by resisting his passes and praises.

More persistent than most, he's determined to show

you that life is better by his side. He comes in strong, he's impressive, and he's everywhere. He's "caught by you," "mesmerized," he's convinced you that "you're different from other women." He does whatever he can to pursue you.

It feels a little too much too soon, but hey, he's actually doing what the other men won't. He "knows what he wants," and he won't rest until he gets you. It's impressive!

Eventually, after the barrage of his continued efforts, you give in. You show interest in him. And before you know it, you're all in, too. Things still feel a little off, and you still feel a bit nervous around him. But this guy has been after you for a while! Is it finally safe to say he's in it for the right reasons? He treats you like the only woman in the room. Except now that he knows you're interested, you're back to being one of many, one who will have to fight for his time and attention, another piece on his game board. You're too invested now to back out, and he's showing you just enough to make you think his investment is because you are something special to him. Just enough to make you believe he's actually interested at all. And this interest will pop up every time he needs you: maybe physically, maybe for money, perhaps just for an ego boost.

Unfortunately, the only person supremely important to

him is himself. And he is about to prove that to you time and time again. You've fallen for a narcissist, and from here on out, life is all about him! Life is all about what you can give him and how long he can keep you believing that you got drawn into any kind of a good deal. You fell for a narcissist, and it's all downhill from here!

By the time you realize it, a lot of time may have passed. It may be weeks, months, or even years before you realize that he is only ever looking out for himself. His interest in you is solely for whatever validation you can provide him.

What can you do now? Well, it's time to regain control of your life and learn to heal yourself. If you are clueless about where to start, then you are in the right place. This book will help you improve your understanding of the situation, and as you understand yourself better, you can make better life choices. You can evaluate the reasons you keep getting into these types of relationships, the kind of guys you keep getting attracted to, and the role you play in it all.

As you learn this, it will become easier to make

changes, take back control of your life, and form healthier patterns of relating.

The truth is, it might not be easy to break free of a narcissistic relationship. Unless you understand how a narcissist operates, getting away from a toxic relationship will not be simple. However, it could be one of the best decisions you ever make.

How do I know? Well, I have had personal experience in dealing with problematic relationships, both for myself and for those close to me. I have personally had to negotiate my way out of some less than healthy relationship situations. I have had to make the hard decision to choose what I knew was best for me, rather than what was comfortable or easy to do at the time.

I spent several years going through my own journey of self-awareness and emotional healing, which was so liberating for me. I felt like a different person on the other side of it.

I also have had to accompany those dear to me through similar journeys in their own lives. As a mother of two daughters, I have had to help them negotiate the painful landscape of first loves and wrong relationships, as they have grown and discovered who they are.

All this has given me a thorough knowledge of narcissists and how to deal with them. I believe that the insight I have gained is invaluable for anyone who wants to learn about healing themselves after a narcissistic relationship.

You may feel stuck where you are right now, but one undeniable truth about life is that change is constant. Nothing in life ever stays the same. So, even if you feel that you are stuck in a dark space right now, know that it will change; you will get out of it. With a little effort, consistency, and patience, you *can* change your life for the better.

By understanding yourself and learning what type of people to stay away from, you can start forming and developing healthier and happier relationships. If you want to live a better life, then it's only a decision away. You are the only one that can change your life, and you can do it.

By using the simple, yet practical tips in this book, you can empower yourself, set some boundaries, gain control of your life, and dictate how you want your relationships to be.

Your life doesn't have to be an endless stream of unsatisfying relationships. You are not doomed, and you don't have to live wondering if you are inadequate in any way. If you ever catch yourself thinking like that, don't worry, you are not going crazy, we all feel that way sometimes. But know that you can start living the kind of life you have always wanted. You can have very different relationship experiences. You can experience unconditional love.

All you need to do is give yourself some time. You deserve the same care and compassion you reserve for others. It's okay if it takes you a while to recognize your needs and desires, or strengths and weaknesses. The process doesn't happen overnight. It will take time and some conscious effort. There might be certain parts of the process that make you uncomfortable, but it will be worth it. Trust me; I know how liberating it can be to regain your sense of control. The freedom at the end of this journey is worth every obstacle you might encounter along the way.

You know the saying, "Old habits die hard?" Well, that's true. And every single day that you spend lost in an unhealthy relationship with a narcissist, you are actually strengthening an undesirable habit. The longer you take to distance yourself from the narcissist and empower yourself, the more self-damage you are inflicting. Don't allow yourself to get trapped by inaction.

It's time to finally understand your relationship behavior and gain a better understanding of who you are. Let the healing process begin; there is no time like the present to get started. The kind of deep, loving, and satisfying relationship you always wished for might be just around the corner. The power lies in your hands. So, don't waste another minute, the journey to your romantic future starts today!

PART 1: WHAT IT IS

The first step in dealing with a narcissist is knowing how to recognize one. Unless you understand what narcissism is and what the essential characteristics of a narcissist are, you are at a disadvantage. Having some basic understanding will help you to spot a narcissist more quickly and know how to deal with them. Understanding how they operate and how they choose their victims is essential in being able to respond to them the right way.

As you read, you will undoubtedly recognize patterns in your own relationships - maybe with a romantic partner, a friend, or a family member. Take the time to read this section carefully. The better you can identify the narcissist personality in those around you, the easier it will be to set healthy boundaries for yourself, which we'll talk about later.

1

WHO IS THIS GUY?

We use the term "narcissist" rather casually these days to describe anyone who seems to be full of themselves. However, narcissism is much more than a mere obsession with oneself. Those we judge to be narcissists are usually suffering from a psychological condition called Narcissistic Personality Disorder (NPD).

WHAT IS NARCISSISTIC PERSONALITY DISORDER?

In the field of psychology, Narcissistic Personality Disorder (NPD) is classified as a type of personality disorder, wherein the sufferer has a somewhat inflated sense of self-importance, a dire need for excessive attention, a lack of empathy, and a history of troubled relationships. This grand self-image that they create of themselves in their mind allows them to avoid dealing with their psychological insecurities. But creating and maintaining this *illusion of grandeur* results in dysfunctional behavior.

An individual with NPD can come across as arrogant and self-centered. They display a fundamental lack of empathy toward others, which makes them seem inconsiderate and highly manipulative. Narcissists go to great lengths to maintain their fragile self-esteem, despite the cost to those around them.

NPD is problematic for the sufferer and causes disturbances in various aspects of the individual's life, such as their relationships, their professional life, and even their financial matters. When a narcissist doesn't get treated with the special favor that they believe they deserve or stops being the center of attention, they become incredibly disappointed and unhappy. It makes it very hard for them to maintain and develop healthy and fulfilling relationships.

THE GREEK STORY OF NARCISSUS

We derive the term narcissist from the legend of Narcissus. Narcissus is a prominent figure from Greek mythology. The story goes that he was a remarkably handsome young man who admired himself so much that he fell in love with his own reflection. His name has become immortalized in two ways: as the name of a flowering plant; and as synonymous in describing anyone obsessed with themselves, especially their physical appearance.

Several versions of the legend exist, but the basic is as follows. Narcissus was born in Boeotia, as the son of Cephissus, and a nymph named Liriope. When Narcissus was young, a seer named Teiresias warned his mother that he would live a long life, but only as long as he never recognizes himself. As he grew, Narcissus blossomed into a handsome young fellow in his teenage years. His good looks drew the attention of a female nymph named Echo, who pursued him romantically, but he spurned her advances. She went away heartbroken. Unable to recover from the rejection, she wasted away and died, leaving only her voice behind.

Nemesis, the God of revenge, heard of her plight and decided to punish Narcissus, cursing him to never know true love with another, and fall in love with himself instead.

So one hot summer day, when Narcissus had been out hunting, Nemesis lured him to a pool of water to sate his thirst. Leaning over the water to drink, he caught sight of his reflection, and not recognizing it as himself, immediately fell in love with the face he saw. So enamored by the image he saw, he couldn't look away. He was unable to draw himself away from the pool and stayed there transfixed, never to move from that spot. Eventually, he died from the passion that burned in his heart for himself, and he melted away into the earth, and a flower sprung up from his remains. Thus, the legend of Narcissus, the man, became immortalized in the flower that bears his name.

This mythical story is a cautionary tale of the dangers of not seeing anything outside of yourself and how that can affect your own emotional and physical health. We can also see it as a warning about the importance of avoiding someone who is demonstrating such self-absorbed patterns of behavior.

THE SYMPTOMS AND BEHAVIORS OF NARCISSISM

Depending upon the severity of the disorder, the signs and symptoms displayed by the sufferer can vary significantly from person to person. However, an individual with a narcissistic personality disorder often exhibits many of the following symptoms.

Need for Attention

Narcissists have an exaggerated need for attention and validation. They quickly feel dejected when they don't receive the level of focus they desire from others. Whatever they are doing, they always want to be the center of attention. A narcissist's desire for attention and validation is never-ending, like a black hole. Regardless of how much attention they receive, they are always after more, displaying an insatiable hunger that they can never satisfy.

Superiority

Narcissists tend to have an exaggerated sense of self-importance, which makes them feel superior and entitled. In their mind, there exists a hierarchy in the world with them at the top of the chart. A narcissist believes that he knows the best, that he has absolute power, and that he is always right.

Their outlook towards life is quite black-and-white. In a narcissist's mind, things can be good or bad, right or wrong, and superior or inferior. So, unless the narcissist feels superior to others, they believe it makes them inferior.

Perfectionist

Narcissists desire perfection from everything and everyone, without exception. A narcissist believes he should be perfect, others should be perfect, and life must play out precisely the way he expects. Since this demand of life is unreasonable, he often feels frustrated and dissatisfied. When his experience does not meet his perfect expectations, he becomes moody, miserable, or depressed. A narcissist has a tough time regulating his emotions and behavior.

Control

Narcissists have an extreme need to control everything. Since they are often disappointed with the imperfections they see in life, they try to control as much of it as possible. They not only want life to be controlled but also demand that they are the ones to provide that control. This only fuels their sense of entitlement, and they believe that they know everything.

A narcissist has a specific storyline in his mind, and unless everything plays out according to that storyline, he will not be happy or satisfied. He tries his best to control others, but since life is unpredictable, he cannot always do that. So he may often resort to manipulative tactics to obtain or maintain that control.

Narcissists don't hesitate to take advantage of others to attain their objective. They love monopolizing conversations and looking down on others to make themselves seem superior.

Arrogance

Narcissists often come across as arrogant, boastful, pretentious, and proud or conceited. They not only desire the best of everything but also insist that they deserve the best. However, they secretly harbor feelings of shame, vulnerability, and insecurity, and have a fear of humiliation. In fact, a narcissist's self-image, self-worth, and ego are quite frail. All the negative traits they demonstrate are an attempt at preserving this fragile ego.

Because of this internal fragility, everything starts looking like a threat to a narcissist. Even though they love being the center of attention and receiving praise from others, they are regularly overwhelmed with feelings of shame and anger, and they fear rejection from others. Consequently, they often exaggerate their talents and achievements and keep themselves pre-occupied with fantasies of their perfection.

Lack of Empathy

A narcissist is incapable of displaying empathy or even feeling it. They love being around those who are empathetic, but they are incapable of reciprocating any compassion. They are so self-involved that they fail to understand that others are capable of feelings too. Since a narcissist believes he knows the best, he believes others think as he does.

A narcissist believes he is the epitome of perfection. So, he cannot accept his mistakes or take responsibility when something goes wrong. He will always be looking for ways in which he can shrug free of responsibility for his problems and blame others instead.

A narcissist doesn't understand what personal boundaries mean and continually crosses the boundaries of others. A narcissist can act like a petulant child who believes he owns everything. So he expects others to want to do whatever he wants to do and is shocked, or even insulted when others say no.

TYPES OF NARCISSISTS

As we already explored, the idea of narcissism originates from the Greek myth of the self-loving Narcissus. However, narcissism is a more complicated issue than just excessive vanity. In the world of psychology, narcissists get classified into two primary types: Grandiose and Vulnerable. When you understand these two types and their essential characteristics, it will become easier to recognize when you are dealing with a narcissist, and how best to respond to them. In this section, we will examine both types.

Grandiose Narcissists

Grandiose Narcissists are quite easy to spot. They are the classic case. They have an inflated sense of self and are quite self-absorbed. A grandiose narcissist truly believes he is a gift from God and doesn't have any doubts about that belief whatsoever.

Therefore, he continually expects others to treat him as if he is incredibly unique, and can become enraged if he doesn't get special treatment. The most prominent traits of a grandiose narcissist are arrogance, entitlement, envy, and exploitative nature.

A grandiose narcissist is incapable of learning from his mistakes, always thinking that he is right, and convinced that he deserves the best in the world. He is also incapable of being empathetic towards anyone else but expects empathy from others. He freely allows his personality traits to guide his decision-making, and only makes decisions that enable him to get something in return.

Typical behaviors

Grandiose Narcissists are also sometimes known as Overt Narcissists. That's because their narcissistic traits can be easily spotted, and they don't make any effort to hide them. An overt narcissist can appear incredibly exciting and alluring. They are good at turning on the charm to get whatever they want. However, once you are in a relationship with one, everything changes. They tend to put their victims on a pedestal to gain the victim's trust. Once they have this trust, the power dynamic in the equation shifts so that the narcissist has all the power. You can never expect an even playing field in a relationship with an overt narcissist. They think that the rules of life don't apply to them, so they keep changing the rules to suit themselves. They will stop at nothing to get what they want.

Grandiose narcissists appear to exhibit a rather strong sense of self-confidence and self-control, but they are going through life with their heads in the clouds. Since they consider themselves to be so superior to others, they are not always in touch with reality. Staying in a relationship with a grandiose narcissist can be toxic and damaging, as they can be quite callous and indifferent to others. It can be incredibly difficult to expect any rational behavior from a narcissist who continually demands that not only is he the best at everything, but he expects special treatment from everyone around him because of it.

Vulnerable Narcissists

Vulnerable Narcissists are quite the opposite of Grandiose Narcissists. Whereas Grandiose Narcissists have extroverted or "overt" personalities, Vulnerable Narcissists have introverted or "covert" personalities. The "overts" have their traits clearly evident to anyone who spends a fair amount of time around them. But the "coverts," keep their narcissistic traits a little closer to their chest, and so are more difficult to recognize at first.

A Vulnerable Narcissist is characterized by their emotional background. Just like a grandiose narcissist, they are also self-centered, but the reason for this is quite different. A vulnerable narcissist's self-centeredness stems from unreasonable fears that he is worthless and shameful to a certain degree. They are often preoccupied with irrational fears of rejection or abandonment. These unaddressed fears make them oscillate between feelings of *superiority* and *inferiority* based on whatever is going on in their lives at a specific moment.

The difference between a vulnerable narcissist and a grandiose narcissist presents mainly in the different outward display of their emotional wounds. Whereas a Grandiose Narcissist is brash and controlling, a Vulnerable Narcissist often displays constraint, an appearance of empathy, and extreme shyness. But underneath lies a secret core based around the same belief of superiority and the same unrealistic expectations of entitlement. They don't outwardly display the idea that they deserve everything or that they are better from everyone else. However, internally they still feel superior and maintain a protective shell around them to enable them to hold onto those feelings of superiority. This fragile shell can easily collapse, and under it lies an individual who feels easily threatened and is often distressed.

When a vulnerable narcissist's shell gets fractured, it leaves him feeling exposed to those underlying fears that he isn't good enough. This individual might experience shame, depression, panic, anxiety, worthlessness, or any other intense negative emotions. A grandiose narcissist believes that his inner self is authentic and correct; therefore, he never needs to second-guess himself. Whereas a vulnerable narcissist's self-belief is not strong, and so he will continually be in a state of inner turmoil, causing him to hide.

For example, a grandiose narcissist probably uses social media for demonstrating his self-proclaimed excellence or perfection, whereas a vulnerable narcissist will shy away from any such outward expressions. Instead, a covert narcissist might come across as being smugly superior, passive-aggressive, socially distant, and emotionally detached from those around him.

Typical behaviors

Forming a relationship with a vulnerable narcissist is quite easy, but staying in one can be hard. We all tend to suffer from self-esteem issues once in a while or feel overlooked by those around us. But vulnerable narcissists harbor a lot of fear within them. So, their emotional state can oscillate between extreme happiness and misery, depending on whether their self-worth is maintained or not. If anything threatens their value, they can quickly withdraw into their shell. This kind of behavior can make them seem cold and distant.

Just as with grandiose narcissists, covert narcissists lack empathy. Maintaining a relationship with such a narcissist is problematic since they always complain about how unfair the world is to them while requiring plenty of reassurance, which can make them seem rather pitiful.

REASONS WHY PEOPLE BECOME NARCISSISTS

So, how does an individual develop Narcissistic Personality Disorder (NPD)? As with any other psychological disorder, many different factors can contribute. The most common being the experience of their childhood and upbringing. The various parental styles that a child gets exposed to during their formation can have a considerable influence on how they behave as adults. Those who become narcissists may themselves have grown-up with narcissistic or over-controlling parents, or have felt devalued in some significant way in their formative years. In this section, we will look at the most common scenarios where a child might develop NPD.

Narcissistic Parents

If a child is brought up by a parent that is a narcissist, they can turn into a narcissist themselves later in life. When a parent is a narcissist, the children are raised in an environment that is incredibly competitive, to the degree of being toxic.

In such a family, rewards or praise are not bestowed unless there is an outstanding achievement. Love and acceptance are not given just for "being," just for existing; they must be earned. So, a child growing in such a household is praised and showered with attention only when they win something. If they don't achieve, they will become the source of extreme disappointment to their narcissistic parents(s). This type of upbringing causes the child to believe that love is not freely bestowed but is always conditional.

Such a child doesn't understand what stability means. In their bid to try and please their parents, they often ignore their own needs and desires. This kind of conditioning enables them to expect the same from others. It turns them into narcissists who are incapable of loving anyone unconditionally unless the other person does everything the narcissist demands.

Devaluing Parents

An overbearing, domineering, or devaluing parent rarely hesitates in putting their child down. This kind of narcissistic parent not only has unrealistically high expectations of his child but is easily irritable and angered. If there are two or more children in such a household, the parent tends to praise one while devaluing the others. The subject of this praise isn't fixed and can shift from one child to another, depending on the parent's needs. Children who grow up in such dysfunctional households can feel inadequate, angry, and humiliated. There are different ways in which they tend to react to that upbringing. They can become defeated, or angry, or rebellious.

- A defeated child is someone who merely gives up and accepts the fact that they can never win. During their teenage years, they can spiral into depression based on self-hate and shame.
- A rebellious child often goes out of his way to prove his parents wrong and may, in turn, try to devalue them in reprisal for having been devalued by them. Proving that he is special would be his only motive, but it can turn him into a narcissist.
- An angry child can grow up to be furious at the devaluing parent. Anyone who reminds him of his parents in any way would become the unwitting target of his unrequited anger. He not only tries to achieve success but also strives to destroy anyone who threatens his progress. These individuals can turn into toxic or malignant narcissists.

Exhibitionist Narcissist Parents

If one or both parents tend to be exhibitionist narcissists, then the child can also subsequently develop narcissistic traits. An exhibitionist narcissistic parent is someone who offers rewards and praises only if his children are subservient to him. So, a child automatically learns narcissistic values while being discouraged from exhibiting himself or gaining any admiration from others. The child is expected to place his narcissistic parent on a pedestal without questioning their greatness, or ever surpassing that greatness themselves.

When children grow up in such households, they can become covert narcissists. The child is always expected to support the ego of his exhibitionist parent and not get praise himself. So, when the child grows up, he has self-esteem issues and becomes uncomfortable when put in the spotlight, while all the time he secretly desires praise from others.

Golden Child Treatment

Covert narcissistic parents are also uncomfortable being in the spotlight themselves, but still want to feel special. One way they overcome this is by living vicariously through the attention given to their children. They start indulging in excessive bragging about how talented their child is. The child is usually gifted in some way and rightly deserves some praise, but these parents push this to extremes.

Excessive idealization that a child is flawless or exceptional can cause the child to develop narcissistic tendencies later in life. When parents unreasonably idealize their child, the child starts believing they are lovable only if they are perfect and worthy of the love they crave. This expectation, that love is conditional, can make them form unrealistic expectations for themselves, not just about how to behave, but also about love in general. Such a child might feel ashamed whenever he notices any flaws in himself because his parents idealize him. So, the child starts striving for perfection and seeks out any evidence that enables him to prove he is flawless.

While dealing with this, a child might lose touch with his real self and become incapable of discerning his real personal likes or dislikes. Instead, he starts exploring the idea of the kind of person he is *supposed to be* to deserve his parents' love and tries to become that instead, which can lead to stunted emotional development.

2

WHY ME?

It's a popular misconception that narcissists often look for individuals who are weak because they are easier to manipulate. However, that is not the case. Rather than being attracted to weak characters, they get drawn toward strong, healthy people. Individuals targeted by narcissists often have healthy relationships, good family bonds, successful careers, or other strengths that put them in the limelight.

- They are attracted to individuals who are strong-willed and have certain traits or talents they admire.
- They befriend those with natural beauty or exceptional ability in certain areas of life.

- They go after those that seem to be better than others at various creative or sporting skills.
- They seek out those with high emotional intelligence, individuals with high sensitivity to the emotions and needs of others around them.

Narcissists often have unrealistic expectations of what they desire from a relationship and potential partners, which means the narcissist always ends up in unhappy relationships once the initial charm wears off. He wants his partner to flatter him and puff up his prize, but once his partner realizes that he is human and has flaws, it spoils his chance to appear perfect. So he turns on her. For a narcissist, a relationship is not a source of joy or satisfaction. Instead, it's a source of control. He feels better when he has complete control over his partner and the relationship.

So, if a narcissist partners with an individual who takes good care of herself and is calm and happy, he derives pleasure from watching her fall apart. When a confident and composed woman becomes a blubbering mess, a narcissist feels good. Yes, it's as evil as it sounds.

Let's look at some of these personality traits and look at why narcissists are attracted to them.

THE TALENTED OR BEAUTIFUL

Narcissists often target people who are simply good looking. Anyone who is in good shape, takes care of their health, exercises a lot, or takes pride in their appearance can be a potential target. Likewise, anyone who has a notable talent in an area such as music, or dance or sports, can also be a target. Anything that makes them noteworthy or makes them stand out among the general population can make them a target. The narcissist may not consciously set out to seek after such people, but gets drawn to them like a-moth-to-the-flame because of their strengths.

Why is this so? Well, since the narcissist has a compulsive need to prove himself as superior, it is a more significant ego boost to prove himself superior to a strong, healthy personality rather than a weak one. Then when the narcissist finally manages to tear down his strong victim, he feels doubly accomplished and satisfied. All those with a narcissistic personality disorder want to feel good about themselves, so they naturally gravitate towards those who can help them feel that way.

There are two ways in which a narcissist can feel good about himself, but with both, his aim is always to make himself feel special or superior.

The first is simply by hanging out with those who are talented or beautiful. He basks in the light of their glory and feels accomplished just by association with them. He thinks *he* is "somebody" because of who *they* are.

The second way is to experience feelings of power is by putting down someone who is physically more attractive or emotionally and mentally stronger than himself. He likes to triumph over others to stroke his ego, making himself feel superior by making others feel inferior. When he manages to better them and break their spirit, he proves his superiority to himself. This natural tendency is present in all narcissists, regardless of how hard they try to mask it.

They will always befriend those who represent a challenge for them. It's a strange compliment, but whatever strength you have that makes you notable or desirable, is what attracts the narcissist to you.

EMPATHS

One of the basic principles of physics states that opposites attract. We were all taught this in school. Remember how it is only the opposite poles of a magnet that attract one another? Well, this stands true, not just in physics but in many other aspects of life, including dating and relationships.

In a healthy relationship, this can be a good thing. When two opposite personalities come together for the right reasons, the unique traits of each partner combine to help complete each other. Each partner benefits from what the other brings to the relationship. However, when individuals who are poles apart are drawn together for the wrong reasons, it can be a recipe for disaster. For instance, we are often attracted to others who will help us meet our needs. But if these needs are selfish, and happen to include constant praise and validation, that can make for an unbalanced pairing. But this is really what the narcissist is after, so they often end up pursuing individuals with a high level of empathy.

Empaths and narcissists lie on the opposite ends of the emotional spectrum. Empathy is the ability to not only understand what another person is feeling but also to understand the reason *why* they feel the way they do. Empaths exhibit this beautiful trait to a high level of maturity, whereas narcissists are entirely devoid of it. An individual with a narcissistic personality disorder thrives on the need for validation and admiration. Since empaths are highly sensitive individuals who are in tune with other's emotions, they can sense the narcissist's need for praise and admiration.

It's an empath's inherent desire or tendency to make

others feel better. A narcissist needs constant attention, praise and validation to feel better. So, an empath is an ideal person to give the narcissist precisely what he wants.

In some ways, Empaths are like emotional sponges who tend to absorb the emotions and feelings of those around them. This is alluring to a narcissist because it seems they have finally found someone who seems eager to fulfill all their needs, quite selflessly. A narcissist views an empath as a loving, caring, and devoted individual who will do everything she can to make the narcissist feel good about himself.

But in the long term, the attraction between a narcissist and an empath is a recipe for disaster and quickly becomes quite toxic. A narcissist will have complete control in such a relationship since an empath's fundamental nature makes her hard-wired to meet the needs she senses in her partner, whatever they are.

When an empath feels attracted to a narcissist, they are actually being attracted to his false self, a personality that he wears like a mask. Narcissists never show their true selves, at least initially. Instead, they take some time to gain and build their victim's trust. They are capable of turning on the charm, and they can keep up the pretense of a false self so that they appear intelligent, charming, and understanding. This façade lasts until they have gained their victim's trust. Then at some point in the relationship, they start to show their true colors and can become quite cold. The person that seemed so attractive and attentive now seems distant, callous, manipulative, and selfish.

The narcissist's pattern is that when he is trying to reel someone in, he will always seem loving and attentive. During the initial stages, he will make his victims only see his good qualities and make them believe the relationship is for their good. But since narcissists are filled with contempt and view others as inferior, this rosy phase doesn't last. Once the narcissist starts seeing his partner's flaws, he will no longer idealize her and will begin blaming her for her shortcomings.

All empaths believe they can fix the problems others have and solve or heal anything with love and compassion. They think that if they just listen more or give more, they can help others. But regardless of how hard an empath tries, a narcissist's needs can never be satisfied. The more an empath gives, the more a narcissist will demand. It's a never-ending vicious cycle that, in the long term, will only harm the empath's wellbeing.

Harmony

Empaths love peace and harmony, whereas narcissists produce drama and chaos. Empaths work rather hard to maintain unity, whereas narcissists thrive in disarray, and delight in pulling others' strings. Narcissists enjoy manipulating empaths and stringing them along by showing some intermittent hope. By showing them occasional kindness or showering them with some compliments, it only makes it harder for the victim to break free of the narcissist's grip. Since the victim gets intermittent hope, she convinces herself that if only she behaved properly, did certain things, or said the right words, then all would be well.

If you are dealing with a narcissist, this pattern might sound quite familiar to you. A narcissistic partner might convince you that you merely need to change your attitude and behavior to make the relationship work. However, it's nothing more than a manipulative tactic.

Empaths understand that we are all humans, have some flaws, and so are patient and willing to encourage someone else's personal growth. They don't mind giving others a chance even if they got hurt in the past. As soon as the narcissist says, "I will try to be better," "I want to change, and I am trying to change," "I know I am not perfect, and I am sorry," or anything else along those lines, an empath will always give him another chance. An empath wrongly believes that the narcissist is admitting his fault. However, the narcissist is merely trying to test the empath's boundaries to understand what he can get away with. It's a simple manipulative tactic that narcissists employ to exploit their empathetic partners.

Trauma Bond

The basic push-pull nature of a narcissistic relationship creates a trauma bond between the abuser and the victim. The empath understands that she's not perfect and has flaws herself, so she is always willing to look at another's faults and accept them. A narcissist thoroughly exploits this ability. Whatever behavior he dishes out, the empath just questions herself and starts looking at her own behavior to figure out things she can change. The victim starts believing that it's impossible to let go of the relationship, regardless of the damage inflicted. The narcissist gets away with all his undesirable behavior since the empath is busy blaming herself.

Sentimentality

If you are an empath, your sentimentality enables you to love another person genuinely. However, this trait becomes an enticing target for a narcissist. The twisted mind of a narcissist enables him to use your sentimentality against you. By overwhelming you with affection during the initial stages, he secures your trust; because he knows that once he has done so, your sentimentality will get the better of you. He will effectively create happy memories during the initial stages because he knows you will hold onto those happy moments when the relationship starts taking a toxic turn. Keep in mind that all he's doing is toying with your emotions. He knows he can pull your heartstrings and will do so to keep a firm hold on the relationship.

Resilience

Your ability to get back on your feet and move past a traumatic incident shows your resilience. A narcissist always uses his victim's resilience against them to perpetuate the cycle of narcissistic abuse. For instance, individuals who have overcome any trauma or violence in their past become ideal targets for the narcissist and other emotional predators. Since the narcissist is aware that you managed to survive all the hardships life threw your way and were able to bounce back from it, he thinks of it as a sign that he can treat you any way he wants and get away with it.

He knows that your resilience will allow you to stay in the relationship regardless of the adversities that come your way. This show of strength will become your weakness. If you have a high degree of resilience, it's quite likely you will not give up on the relationship, even after an abusive episode. Even if you detect any potential threats, you overlook these red flags and fight your instinct to flee because of your past. You might also reach a stage where you start believing that the only way to make your narcissistic partner love you is by enduring all of his narcissistic abuse.

Conscience

Conscientious individuals think about other's welfare rather than just their own, sticking stick by their promises and doing their best in every situation, regardless of the outcome. As long as she has a clear conscience, such a woman would not hesitate to stand her ground.

Conscience is the driving force that enables you to discern between good and evil, the right decision, or the wrong decision. It's your moral compass that ensures you are doing the right thing. Conscience is an incredibly valuable trait, but a narcissist will weaponize it. It's a trait that a lot of emotional predators look for in their victims. Since your conscience inherently guides your decisions, you might naïvely believe that others also follow their conscience as you do. This kind of naive thinking is a sign of the purity of your heart and mind. However, for an emotional predator such as a narcissist, it is an incredibly easy trait to manipulate in his victims.

A narcissist is well aware of the fact that your conscience will prevent you from blaming him for his mistakes and that he will always be given the benefit of the doubt. He knows he can get a second chance. Since he's aware of it, he will utterly exploit it. So, the primary conscience that enables you to make the right decisions in life will effectively be used against you.

Integrity

Integrity represents your ability to follow through in your obligations, and stick to any promises you make. It is another trait that makes you an attractive target to a narcissist. Narcissists are often devoid of all sense of morality and prey on their target's integrity to meet their selfish needs. For instance, you may believe it's not morally right to end a relationship, even if your partner cheats on you. If this is the case, your narcissistic partner may exploit your integrity by indulging in affairs, knowing that you will forgive him and stick to your promises to love him because of your integrity. But this is just exploitation and another way that narcissists take advantage of their victims.

SUMMARY

If you notice any of these patterns, it's a sign that you may be in a narcissistic relationship. Try to understand that your narcissistic partner is merely exploiting you to meet his selfish needs and desires. He doesn't care about the relationship or your personal growth. All that he cares about is himself, and regardless of what you do, you cannot satisfy his needs. Understand that this kind of relationship is extremely unhealthy and will likely end in major heartbreak and disappointment.

PART 2: HOW IT PLAYS OUT

So far, we have looked at some fundamental traits of narcissists and their typical victims. Recognizing those basic traits can help you understand the reasons why they target specific types of people and make it easier for you to avoid narcissists in the future.

In this section, we will look at what a relationship with a narcissist actually looks like. Hopefully, this may help you identify some different signs or behaviors you might be experiencing, but overlooking. Your love for your narcissistic partner can blind you to the issues and make you ignore the red flags, even if they are right in front of you.

So let's get started, and look more closely at how a relationship with a narcissist plays out.

3

THE PATTERN OF A NARCISSISTIC RELATIONSHIP

When you are in a relationship with a narcissist, it can feel like you are on a rollercoaster ride. You ride the extreme highs and lows, not knowing what is coming next. Dealing with a partner whose persona keeps shifting depending on his mood, can make you feel tired and frustrated. He can be a real Dr. Jekyll and Mr. Hyde. You can end up feeling extremely confused and unsure of yourself and the relationship in general.

A romantic relationship is supposed to be about love. It should satisfy our basic need to receive love and to give love, to experience a connection with another person. These are the reasons why people get into relationships. However, this doesn't apply to a relationship with a narcissist. Since they are so self-absorbed, the giving of love isn't one of the reasons why a narcissist enters relationships. They get into relationships to receive only. They lack empathy, so it makes it exceedingly difficult for a narcissist to truly ever connect with another individual.

Regardless of whether they are an overt or a covert narcissist, they share a commonality: they *need* people! Individuals with narcissistic personality disorder are self-absorbed, but they need people more than anyone else. Why? Because their fragile self-esteem and self-worth aren't built internally but stem from external sources.

Unless a narcissist receives constant praise and attention from others, he cannot survive. He continually needs people to fan the embers of his personality. As mentioned in the previous chapter, a narcissist's need for attention and praise is like a black hole. There is an enormous void that is perpetually present within all narcissists. A narcissist can try filling this void with love and esteem shown by others, but since it's like a bottomless pit, it can never truly be filled.

It almost seems like a narcissist's mind is continually seeking something. He might not know what it's looking for, but he is undoubtedly never happy with whatever he has. Nothing he does will ever satisfy him, and nothing will be close to perfection. This attitude not only makes narcissists self-absorbed, but it also makes them oblivious to the needs and wants of others around them.

These two characteristics, when combined, make a narcissist incapable of ever truly, and unconditionally loving someone else outside of himself. So, why does a narcissist enter into relationships if he cannot truly love someone else? Well, he does it for selfish reasons. A narcissist might believe that a relationship could help fill the constant void he feels. Also, it gives him an external source to produce a continuous supply of things he needs. Whenever he is running low on self-esteem, he can always turn to his partner for a quick fix. For all attention needs, from sex to just having a person to massage his ego, a relationship is an excellent way for a narcissist to get all his needs met.

All narcissists share essential characteristics that cause them to be exploitative and manipulative. So most narcissistic relationships follow a specific pattern. There are three primary phases that a narcissistic relationship goes through. They are the idealization phase, the devaluation phase, and the discard phase. As you read through this chapter, you may recognize this pattern in your relationship.

THE IDEALIZATION PHASE

Once a narcissist finds himself drawn toward someone, all his energy, attention, and focus will be directed towards that person. Narcissists tend to become extremely vigilant while pursuing their target and manage to create a facade of perfection that they know will appeal to them. A narcissist will try projecting himself to be someone that he knows the victim desires.

So, during the initial stage, a narcissist is extremely caring, attentive, and loving. He comes on strong. He will start showering his victim with praise and compliments and will do everything possible to sweep her off her feet. The first stage is, therefore, known as the idealization or over-evaluation stage.

Narcissists essentially place their targets on a pedestal, start idealizing and worshipping them. They will go to great lengths to make their target feel like they are the best thing that has ever happened to them. The narcissist is euphoric and ecstatic in the first stage of the relationship. He will be full of hopes, dreams, and have a sparkle in his eyes. He will regularly talk to his victim. Every relationship goes through a honeymoon phase, but this is at another level altogether. In this stage of the relationship, the narcissist says and does everything possible to make his victim feel like she has finally found her soulmate, her prince charming.

He appears so charismatic and presents himself as everything you always desired. Even if he seems a little self-absorbed, he is the life of the party. You cannot ignore his charm, and he swiftly sweeps you off your feet. He is trying to lower your guard. He is trying to earn your trust, build hopes for a future, and create some happy memories. Why does he do all these things? He does this because this is the pattern he follows: he always starts new relationships this way.

By doing so, he is giving you some happy moments to hold onto when the abuse starts, and the relationship starts unraveling. Also, this is probably as close to the feeling of love a narcissist might ever get. This first stage of idealization might seem like infatuation and obsession to someone with a rational mind.

You will be so caught up in all this attention; you will start to think you found the perfect partner. The narcissist will be exactly all that you ever wanted in a man. He does this by mirroring all the things he knows appeals to you. The more he learns about you and the type of person that appeals to you, he becomes that. As he showers you with all this attention and love, you are inclined to ignore any of the red flags you might have normally noticed. However, with narcissists, the one thing that you can never prepare for yourself is the next stage that follows.

The idealization can last anywhere from a few weeks to several months, depending on the kind of narcissist you're dealing with. This time frame usually depends on how long he needs to ensure that he has successfully secured your unconditional love and devotion. Sadly, all that you witnessed during the previous phase was a facade. You were interacting with the narcissist's false self, and you have yet to become acquainted with the real him.

Then, when you least expect it, comes the second phase of a narcissistic relationship: the devaluation phase.

THE DEVALUATION PHASE

One day everything is fine, and the next, nothing seems to be the way it was used to be. The euphoric and heady high the narcissist experienced during the previous stage slowly starts fading away. This is when your charming suitor's mask finally comes off, and cracks start appearing in his facade. He stops making as much effort as he previously did to secure his false self. Instead, he starts reducing his efforts and begins to reveal his true colors.

During this second stage, he starts displaying extreme

mood swings, becomes easily agitated, and starts blaming you for the slightest of mistakes. Even if you did nothing wrong, he would blame you for the way the relationship has turned. He will start disappearing quite frequently and give you the silent treatment whenever you try to bridge the distance between the two of you. As he starts withdrawing, it can become quite difficult for you to stay grounded in the relationship. After all, the rosy honeymoon phase was quite good, and you were starting to think about a future together. But as soon as you began thinking like that, he started withdrawing, causing you to try and cling onto him.

And that is what he wanted. When the victim starts clinging onto the narcissist, it puts him in a position of power. You become the unwitting pawn in the narcissist's gameplay. Now that he has you under his thumb, he knows that you will cater to all his needs and demands. You will start doing whatever he wants because you want the relationship to last. Your care comes from a place of love. Whereas, the narcissist is merely there to exploit all the attention he gets. The more you try to cling on, the more the narcissist starts pulling away. He will blame and criticize you for everything. You end up becoming an emotional punching bag for the narcissist. Understandably, at this point, you may feel like a nervous wreck.

At this point, the narcissistic partner will have given you no explanation. You are probably trying to work out how everything was fine and dandy one minute, and now all that you hoped for is hanging in the balance. But what happened was that, previously, he was merely projecting an image of what he thought would attract you. Now he has revealed his true personality. The person you fell in love with doesn't exist, and it was merely a façade he put up to secure you, his source of supply.

You need to prepare yourself for dealing with the narcissist's words, behaviors, and actions during this stage. As the victim tries to cling onto the false personality that they fell in love with, the narcissist starts doling out abuse to fulfill his need to feel superior. Even if he makes a mistake, he will not accept any responsibility for it. If that causes you to hurt, then too bad, because he isn't capable of loving anyone other than himself. If you are wondering why he doesn't seem to care about how he is treating you or why he doesn't validate your feelings, then it's because he never genuinely cared about you. The relationship until now was just a means for the narcissist to meet his needs.

A narcissist will make you believe that love is conditional. As long as you do and say certain things, you will receive some praise from him. By giving you intermittent hope, he is merely manipulating you to get what he wants from you without a fight. All this mental manipulation is deliberate. He is doing this to keep you hooked onto the relationship while he looks for his new target. Also, it makes you more susceptible to comply with his unreasonable demands. He becomes oblivious and indifferent to any hurt you might be experiencing.

Narcissists are good at projecting their emotional turmoil onto others. That is one of the reasons why you become his emotional punching bag. He feeds off your misery, even when he is the reason for it. His cruel, unsettling, and indifferent attitude can leave you thoroughly confused.

Narcissists get bored after a while, and that is what starts to happen during this stage. He slowly appears to be losing his interest in you. A child gets bored after playing with the same toy for a while. And in the same way, the narcissist also slowly loses interest in you. Remember the void that we mentioned a while ago? Well, that void starts gradually reappearing. He will start questioning your worthiness and start behaving as if you are not as "special" as he thought you were. After all, if you were special, then the void would not have returned. This is precisely what a narcissist thinks.

THE DISCARD PHASE

The shift from the second stage to the third phase can be gradual but is more likely to be very sudden, even overnight. Once you have served your purpose or your usefulness has run its course, the narcissist will discard you, abruptly and without warning.

In fact, it's somewhat baffling to note the ease with which he can pull away. In the twinkling of an eye, all the attention that he was giving you, whether it was good or bad, will be gone: replaced with indifference, silence, and a coldness, bordering on callousness.

Don't be surprised if you don't hear from your narcissistic partner for days or weeks at a time. He will probably stop returning your phone calls, or even when he does, it will always be after a delayed response. All the promises he made in the previous stage are broken. You might start suspecting that he is involved with someone else during this period. Feelings of confusion and inadequacy are bound to crop up. You might start wondering where you went wrong and what you have done to cause the relationship to unravel.

Those who are not familiar with the narcissistic personality disorder might be at a total loss to understand how callous a narcissist can be. A narcissist can easily pull away and walk away from a relationship.

The reality is that, to him, you were nothing more than an object with a fixed period of usefulness. Once the object serves its purpose or if he no longer finds it useful, he will simply discard it. The "I love you" and "I love you not," charade will keep going on for as long as it suits the narcissist's needs. Then he simply walks out of your life.

He may periodically return, and keep walking in and out of your life as if nothing ever happened. But once the narcissistic relationship finally comes to a real end, the victim is left wondering what they did wrong. If you are in this stage, you might ask yourself questions like, "Did he even love me?" Or "Did this relationship mean anything to him?" The simple answer to this question is no. No, he never loved you. For him, the relationship was just a means to an end.

Getting over a narcissist can be difficult. Their victims often turn into emotional wrecks, whose self-esteem has been demolished by the devaluing and demeaning behavior that he subjected them to. Depending on how long it was before they managed to break free of the relationship, the time required to repair the damage of the narcissistic abuse can be extensive. Victims of such relationships often turn into mere shadows of their former selves until they learn to trust themselves again.

As a victim of narcissistic abuse, never blame yourself.

While you are trying to put all the pieces back together, you need to keep in mind that he deliberately targeted you. You were regularly lied-to and manipulated by a con artist. It's not your fault: a narcissist always repeats these patterns with all his victims.

Once the relationship is over, it's time to break free of the hurt and take time out to recover and heal. It might be some time until you are ready to shut the door on that period of your life and move on.

In the following three chapters we will explore these three stages in more detail and examine some things to look out for.

4

THE IDEALIZATION STAGE

In the previous chapter, we briefly looked at an overview of the three stages that a typical narcissistic relationship goes through. Now let's take a more detailed look at the first stage.

This phase of "idealization" is the first part of a narcissist's manipulative cycle when he works hard to woo you and get you successfully under his influence. It's an exciting romantic time that precedes any hint of abuse or mistreatment, such a wonderful time, the memories of which you try and hold on to when things start to go downhill.

THE LOVE BOMB

In the beginning, the narcissist does everything he possibly can to sweep you off your feet. He treats you like royalty. You feel like a princess. You start thinking that this is everything you have ever wanted or desired. You begin to believe that the fairytale romance you hoped for since childhood is slowly playing out in front of your eyes. Your new partner appears to be everything you ever wanted in a man.

But really, he is just presenting himself as the person he perceives that you want him to be. He is molding himself to be your ideal match, the perfect partner you have always desired.

From your side, everything this guy says and does seem to be ideal. But from his viewpoint, he is just playing with a new toy - albeit a shiny new one. It might sound a little harsh, but really, that's what exactly you are to him - a shiny new toy. What happens when a young child gets a new toy? He stops playing with his old toys and starts focusing all his time and attention on playing with the new one. Likewise, a narcissist does the same and concentrates all his attention on you.

Idealization is all about obsession. It might look like love, but it's not real love. It's all about an unhealthy fixation. A stable, mature, and loving individual never obsesses, because obsession is not a trait of a sophisticated, emotionally balanced individual.

Narcissists lean towards obsession since it allows them to avoid or overcome their inner feelings of loneliness, emptiness, and self-deficiency. Narcissists require attention and approval, and plenty of it. These things are not a sign of an emotionally mature individual. Rather, they are an expression of an immature adult or a man-child who doesn't know how to deal with his inner wounds, one that relies on the security that others provide for him. What better way for a narcissist to get this than from a new relationship where two individuals become fascinated with one another? So you become the object of his fascination, the apple of his eye.

In this early phase of your relationship, there are plenty of sweet surprises and sugary compliments. This new man in your life will swoon over you. He will say how you are perfect for him in every way and how his previous partners can never measure up to you. He will place you on a pedestal. He will present you with surprise gifts, do thoughtful acts, and talk of romantic trips together. He may even start talking about the future permanence of the relationship. Romantic interactions may be intense. You will both start believing that you have known each other forever and that this relationship will last through the ages.

All these experiences put you at ease, lower your guard, and make you feel comfortable. All this happens because the narcissist has convinced you that what you share is the real deal. However, the pedestal that he has placed you on is nothing but a house-of-cards, that will inevitably topple whenever the wind starts blowing.

Narcissists are very good at convincing themselves about the validity of things that make them feel superior. They thrive on this perceived sense of superiority and look for kind individuals, who cannot say no, or make it easy for the narcissist to get what he wants. Anything that makes the narcissist feel good is more important than the other person's wellbeing or the relationship in general. As long as his ego is satisfied, he will be fine with anything. The greater the source of supply, the better the narcissist feels about himself. But since the narcissist over-magnifies his mental concept of his new partner, the relationship is never sustainable.

Those who unwittingly fall into his web of being idealized often experience a heady and intoxicating high. However, this is nothing but the first euphoric stage of what will turn out to be a chaotic and confusing relationship. While you think that you have finally found your true love, the narcissist is merely planning how he can exploit you. He may even profess true love and gush about how you are both meant to be together forever. All this might seem genuine, but it is far from the truth. It's all part of the script the narcissist has in his mind. He is merely stringing you along to get what he needs. The aim of the game is for him to get his selfish needs met, and you provide that convenience for him.

So, what are the signs to look out for?

WARNING SIGNS

Everything in Common

Your wonderful new man is so amazed about how you seem to share such common interests. You seem to have everything in common. If you love jazz, he loves jazz. If you are a vegan, then he is a vegan too. He will say and do everything he possibly can to make you believe that you both share all the same interests.

Talking about shared interests is a great way to start a conversation and build a rapport with anyone. When you share similar interests, you naturally become more interested in the other person. A narcissist uses this tactic and can push it to the heights of absurdity. He will do everything he can to show that you both have so much in common. You will start believing that you were both cut from the same cloth. A narcissist will spend most of his time listening to you and excitingly responding to whatever you say to make you feel special.

The narcissist will keep doing this until he has you thoroughly convinced that he is the only person you will ever meet, who is so similar to you. He will work hard at ensuring that every aspect of his personality is precisely what you have always been looking for in a potential partner.

Constant Praise

Narcissists love to praise you during this first stage. We all like to be praised and complimented; it makes us feel good. A narcissist knows this and starts using praise to lower his victim's guard.

All the things he praises you for will make you feel beautiful, wanted, and unconditionally loved. You will feel like you never felt before. He will continuously tell you how lucky he is to have met someone like you. He will claim that you are the best thing that has ever happened to him, and you are the most incredible human being he has met in his life.

He will tell you that you possess qualities that make him believe he has found his soulmate. If he ever compares you to his past relationships or previous partners, he will always tell you that you are a cut above the rest. In fact, the praise will be to the extent that you start believing you are perfect too. It becomes difficult to maintain or hold onto your sense of rationalism when your partner puts you on such a lofty pedestal and makes you believe that you are a gift from the universe itself.

Proclamations of Undying Love

It's quite disheartening when your date starts discussing his previous relationships or compares you to his ex. However, with a narcissistic partner, you don't have to worry about any of that during the initial stages. The narcissist will never make any unfair comparisons of you with his ex. He will claim that you are absolutely perfect the way you are and that he loves you unconditionally. All these declarations of love will sweep you off your feet.

The narcissist wants you to believe that you are soulmates and that you are meant to be together. He might even make you believe that finding each other was destiny's plan all along and that it's magic at work. You might hear sentences like, "You complete me," or "You are my soulmate." In fact, don't be surprised if he starts saying all this within a week or two of the start of the relationship. He will tell you that he has never felt this way before with any other person. It might sound like a fairytale, but all these are simple manipulative tactics a narcissist uses to get into your head. Once you give him the leeway, he starts assuming control of the relationship.

A Future Together

Within a few weeks, he might begin proclaiming that he loves you. He might go to the lengths of telling you that he has always loved you and that he was waiting for someone like you to make him feel whole. He might actively start planning for a future together and will get you excited about the same.

Within a month or two, he might start talking about moving in together. You will already be spending so much time together that you ar are practically living together anyway. The talk of long-term plans, marriage, and children will crop up regularly in your discussions. All this talk will continue to make you feel special and lower your guard. At this time, it might feel like the most romantic thing you have ever heard. However, if you take a moment to catch your breath and look at the situation rationally, you will realize how truly absurd it is.

These tactics he is using are primarily manipulative and being used to create an illusion of perfection. The reality is that it's nothing more than a trap. A healthy and normal relationship will progress at a natural rate. It takes time to get to know each other and to understand each other. If you notice that your partner is already making plans about your marriage within a month of starting dating, it's a red flag you should probably not ignore.

Isolation

Gradually, you start spending all your time together. He takes up all your time and becomes the center of your universe. Everything starts to become about him and spending time with him. He subtly discourages you from spending time with others because he wants you all to himself.

You keep avoiding your other social commitments to spend more time with him. You start canceling your plans with friends and other loved ones. Your friends keep waiting for you, but you are busy with him. Your family waits for you, but you bail on some commitments to spend more time with him.

At some point, you start to feel a little isolated. Your social circle starts shrinking until it consists of just you and your new partner. What is happening is that he is isolating you from your support network, those people in your life who usually help you process the events of your life and see sense and balance. By doing this, he has taken you away from your opportunity to question his behavior when it turns.

When this starts to happen, it is a sign that you are coming to the end of this wonderful, romantic honeymoon phase of your relationship, and though you don't realize it - everything is about to change.

REALITY CHECK

At this point, everything sounds and feels perfect. However, keep in mind that so much of it is not actually real. A healthy and lasting relationship never starts with declarations of true love. Love-at-first-sight might exist in some cases, but it is unlikely that you will find eternal love the moment you first meet someone. You cannot quickly decide that you truly, and unconditionally love someone the moment you set your eyes on them.

If something feels too good to be true, then it usually is. If you find yourself thinking that your new partner is the personification of the prince charming from your childhood fairytales, then something might be amiss. If your gut tells you something is off, then it's time to listen to your gut.

In some ways, the start of a narcissistic relationship is like a dodgy sales deal. What you think you are getting upfront is not always what it turns out to be. Therefore, don't ignore the red flags you see. Start reading between the lines of things he says, and make sure you are acting wisely.

SUMMARY

So, in summary, here is a simple checklist you can use to pick up any behaviors that you might have noticed, but never realized might be red flags to the fact that you are being drawn into a relationship with a narcissist.

- You have met a charming and charismatic guy. He seems too good to be true and ticks off all the boxes for all the things you ever wanted in a partner.
- He says he loves you and says he has never met anyone like you.
- He keeps gushing about you and showers you with plenty of praise, love, and compliments.
- He treats you like a princess, and you are smitten.
- He says he wants to spend all his time with you.
- He takes up all your time and becoming the center of your universe.
- You start to feel isolated from your friends and

family as he discourages you from spending time with anyone else.

- You find yourself doing the things he wants to do rather than what you might feel like doing.

If you tick off most or all these things from the list, then beware that your partner may not be all that he seems, and you may be getting caught in a relationship with a narcissist.

5

THE DEVALUATION STAGE

S uddenly, as quickly as it began, the honeymoon phase of the relationship comes to an end.

What started as a whirlwind romance, now starts to fade and appears to be far less than ideal. This charming perfect gentleman suddenly drops the mask he has been wearing and begins to reveal his true colors. As things progress, your life turns into an emotional rollercoaster. This previously happy person now continually changes his mind and has extreme mood swings. The person who was your biggest fan now becomes so critical at times. All this is so confusing for you as you start to wonder what you have done to deserve this. What has happened? Well, your relationship has just moved into the second stage of life with a narcissist: the devaluation, or "put-down" stage.

LIFE ON THE EMOTIONAL ROLLERCOASTER

Just when you think life couldn't get any better, it takes a nosedive. When it felt like nothing in life could ever go wrong, it takes a turn for the worst. Up until now, your life with your new partner has been so perfect, so idyllic. Then one day, he seems upset.

You come home from work or the mall, expecting to tell him all about your day and have him listen so intently as he usually does, stroking your hair as you sip a glass of wine on the sofa. But today, it is different. He seems angry. He looks upset about something, but you can't work out what? He starts questioning you, asking why you have been out so long, even though you are home at the usual time. This is confusing. This doesn't seem like the man you love. So you placate him, you help him to calm down and try and have a normal evening.

The next day, he surprises you with a bunch of flowers to make up for his behavior the night before. He says he doesn't know why he was upset, and he was just being silly. He promises to not behave like that again, and reaffirms his love for you with more of the praise and adulation you have come to expect from him. Phew! That's a relief. You were very confused by his behavior and starting to worry. But now he seems to be back to normal, and for the next few days, he is his old, wonderful self again. Then at the weekend, it happens again. Ouch!

Over the coming weeks, his mood becomes incredibly erratic. He can be happy one day and extremely critical the next. He seems to have developed a split personality, and it almost makes you feel like you are dating Jekyll and Hyde. We all have emotional mood swings, but the ones the narcissist displays are quite extreme. He can swing from one end of the spectrum to the other with ease.

In any normal relationship, there are plenty of disagreements and the occasional argument. That is quite healthy and even desirable for the well-being of the partnership. After all, when two individuals talk about a subject, there should be two different opinions to discuss. In a healthy relationship, arguments serve as a tool to help each partner express themselves in terms of the relationship and establish the boundaries of who they are and what they expect. This helps the relationship grow and allows each partner to feel that they are an important and equitable member of the partnership.

But in a relationship with a narcissist, arguments are not the usual healthy type. They are often one-sided with the narcissist merely establishing his power, trying to exert control over his partner. Experiencing this can come as a shock, especially when he had convinced you that you both had plenty of similarities. And it is all very up and down: one day you might have had a nasty argument, and he would've probably stopped talking to you. Then the next day, everything is okay again, and how it's supposed to be. All of this can be very unsettling.

CRITICAL

The narcissistic partner starts becoming critical of you. This dramatic change in behavior will catch you off guard, being so different from how he treated you before. All the things that he once praised you about, he now starts criticizing. For instance, if he said that he loved how confident you were, he will begin to criticize your confidence and make you start doubting yourself. If he had initially praised you for your ability to say no, he would now react harshly whenever you say no to him.

So, all the things that you thought had attracted him to you will slowly become the pain points in your relationship. The criticism could come in the form of taunts, or pointed jokes made to make you feel small and inconsequential. He will not hesitate to criticize you in front of your loved ones or colleagues, but might then brush it off as saying it was a harmless joke. When you confront him, don't be shocked if you receive replies like, "You cannot take a joke," "I was joking," or "Stop being so sensitive." He claims it was harmless, but it will have hurt you.

The narcissist truly believes that no one is perfect, except him. He is quite good at identifying the faults in others and even better at exploiting them. Narcissists often resort to passive-aggressive behavior, going to great lengths to belittle you through off-handed remarks. The effect of all this constant criticism is that you keep questioning yourself, asking yourself what you have done wrong. When someone keeps questioning your judgment repeatedly, you start believing you are at fault. And when you do, it merely fuels the narcissistic cycle of abuse and exploitation.

All the passive-aggressive comments are his way of putting you down in front of your peers. Why does he do this? For two reasons. Firstly, it enables him to feel superior by making you feel inferior. The second reason is that by making you question yourself and instigating your self-doubt, it gives him better control over the relationship and more power over you.

CONTROL

In a healthy relationship, the playing field is level for both partners. Each has an equal degree of power, and no one is superior or inferior. But in a relationship with a narcissist, these fundamental dynamics go out of the window. He will always be seeking to be the one in control. Narcissists love to be in control, and they cannot bear having it taken away from them. After all, he has a script in his mind, and everything must play out according to that script: he must always be the one in control.

Control doesn't always have to be obvious, and he may even use sneaky tactics to make sure that he retains it. The first sign of him assuming control is that he is the one making all the decisions in the relationship. Whether they are minor or major decisions, he wants to decide for you. From deciding where you should go for the date night to which people you meet, your narcissistic partner will want to choose everything for you. Initially, it might have sounded quite romantic when he took charge and arranged all your dinner dates and other outings. It felt like he was a strong man who knew how to look after you; it felt like he was acting manly. However, after a while, you start to realize that he is just bossy. Any suggestions you make are unwelcome, and it slowly dawns on you that he wants you to have little or no say in what happens.

Everyone is entitled to hold their own opinions. But in a relationship with a narcissist, you soon find that your views don't matter, and he is much happier if you never even express them. Your partner's motto in life seems to be, "My way or the highway." If you do dare to offer your opinion, he goes on the attack. He does everything he possibly can to belittle and devalue your suggestions.

All this rejection of your input, causes you to start doubting your judgment. After a while, you get used to having your ideas shot down, so you refrain from ever expressing your opinion. You become compliant. The narcissist gets his way unchallenged, and you merely go along with whatever he says.

LACK OF CARE

In a regular healthy relationship, both the partners care for each other. Both partners should have a concern about the other's welfare and show interest in helping maintain that welfare. It cannot be a one-way street where one partner is always a care-giver while the other one is only ever a care-receiver. But in a relationship with a narcissist, this is what he expects as the norm.

Your narcissistic partner will always expect you to be at his beck and call. When he is sick, he expects you to be there, to look after him, and nurse him. But when *you* are sick, he is nowhere to be seen. He is busy, or he has other things that he needs to do. Your being sick is a huge inconvenience to him. When he needs you, he expects you to be available; if you aren't there, it can trigger him, and he can get angry. But he is never around when *you* need *him*. You are left to deal with all your problems on your own.

He behaves in this way because he doesn't actually care about your wellbeing. In his head, the relationship is merely a means to an end: that end being his comfort!

MANIPULATION

A narcissist is an emotional predator, and like all emotional predators, he loves manipulation. A narcissist certainly doesn't shy away from using manipulation to get his way. After all, if he showed his true colors during the initial stages of the relationship, you might not have ended up together in the first place. He will do everything he possibly can to keep you with him for as long as it serves his needs. He can seem incredibly charming at times, but all this charm is just his way of holding you where he wants you.

Narcissists are notorious for withholding love whenever they don't get something they want. Withholding is a sign of emotional immaturity, as he is essentially throwing a tantrum, just like a toddler that doesn't get their way. He will give the silent treatment, or just become unreasonable and distant until you give him what he wants.

Eventually, as his unwitting victim, you conclude that as long as you behave and do the things he wants you to do, he will love you, and all will be well. If you keep pleasing him, he will shower you with praise. Whenever he comes up with an outlandish request, you might comply with it because you believe you are doing it out of love for him. However, the moment you stop complying with his demands, the praise and appreciation stop too. It's his way of conditioning you to become his pawn.

Another manipulative tactic is accusation reversal. If you ever decide to confront the narcissist about his behavior, be prepared for how he will react. He will swiftly turn the accusation back onto you. You start off trying to confront him, but you suddenly find yourself on the back foot, defending yourself against the very same thing you were accusing him of. For instance, you might find his behavior too controlling in general, and you try to talk to him about it. When you do, he will quickly turn the conversation around by suggesting that *you* are the one who is extremely controlling and have no trust in the relationship. Or, if you have reason to doubt your partner's fidelity, and you confront him about that, he will immediately question *your* fidelity and accuse you of being the one having an affair. He will always paint himself as the saint in the relationship.

GASLIGHTING

The term "Gaslighting" describes a particular form of abusive behavior whereby the abuser manipulates information in such a way as to make the victim question their own sanity.

This term originates from a stage play called Gas Light written in 1938 by a British dramatist Patrick Hamilton. This play became famous through George Cukor's 1944Hollywood movie, a psychological thriller entitled "Gaslight." This movie stars Ingrid Bergman and Charles Boyer in the leading roles. Boyer portrays the role of a narcissistic husband (Gregory), while Bergman (Paula), his wife, is the victim.

In the movie, Gregory manipulates Paula into thinking that she is slowly going mad. He starts tricking and manipulating her to believe she is stealing unconsciously and that she is hearing voices. By using these manipulative tactics, Gregory gets Paula to start questioning her sanity and think she is losing her mind. This was all done as part of a diabolical plot to steal her expensive family heirloom jewels. If you recognize yourself in Paula's plight, then it may be a sign that you, yourself, are being gaslighted.

The Gaslighter might do things, or have conversations with you about things, that they later deny ever having happened. They might suggest that you imagined it all. They may purposely hide objects from you, and then deny knowing anything about it. They might suggest that you have done something which you have no memory of. You have no memory of it because you didn't do it. The purpose of this behavior is solely to confuse you. If they can get you to distrust your own mind, it gives them a great feeling of power.

Gaslighting is an insidious behavior because it seeks to undermine your trust in yourself, which is the very foundation of your personality.

SHAMING

Shame is an intense and painful feeling stemming from the belief that we are flawed, and therefore, don't deserve acceptance or the chance to experience a sense of belonging. Shame is an incredibly powerful feeling, and a narcissist realizes its power. Guilt and shame are closely linked. Guilt is a sign you are going against your conscience; shame is the self-condemnation you feel for having done so. If you do something you consider to be wrong and are aware of it, you will be ashamed of your behavior. A narcissist knows this and will weaponize shame to use it against you.

Pushing Boundaries

One of the main ways a narcissist manipulates you with shame is by testing and exploiting your boundaries. Most narcissists have a limited concept of personal boundaries themselves. They almost see it as quaint that you have a concept of certain behaviors being right or wrong. To them, any behavior is always justified; if it achieves its aim. To them, the end always justifies the means. So they see the testing of your boundaries almost as a form of entertainment.

There is no subject more susceptible to this boundary-pushing than the area of sex. Rest assured, he *will* try and push your boundaries in regards to sex. He might try and coax you into doing things you are uncomfortable with, things you initially refused to do. You probably think you are complying with his request because you love him, but you are just bending under his pressure. If you notice that you are doing things that you are uncomfortable with, only to please your partner, you really shouldn't ignore it.

Sure, it's okay to keep an open mind and experiment with new things, but not at the cost of your conscience and peace.

Embarrassment

Another way that narcissists use shame is to threaten their victims with embarrassment. They love gathering information about their partner and storing it in their memory for later use - or rather misuse. During the initial stages of the relationship, when you felt that you had found your soulmate, you would have worn your heart on your sleeve. So, it's natural that you might have shared some of your deepest secrets with him at that time. However, the narcissist will use these stories to keep you always-in-check by threatening to expose your secrets. For instance, let's say that on a drunken night in the past, you cheated on your ex, and you once shared this secret with your current narcissistic partner. Then one night, when you are out drinking, he might casually drop this piece of information while conversing with your friends. He exploits your personal information like this just to remind you that he is in a position of power.

. . .

Blaming

A third way that a narcissist can use shame to control you is by painting you with the same brush as him. For example, if you ever mention talking about what is happening in the relationship with others, he will lead you to believe that you look as bad as him since you were involved too. He will be blaming you for doing what he pressured you into. He will start making you feel ashamed for your complicity in doing all the things that he made you do. He does this to discourage you from sharing information about the toxic state of the relationship to outsiders. He is primarily using shame to prolong the unhealthy relationship and continue exploiting you.

EMOTIONAL OVERWHELM

Being in love with a narcissist can be overwhelming. During the initial stage of the relationship, it's quite likely that the narcissistic partner became your only priority. You were probably used to canceling and rescheduling all your plans to spend more time with him. He was doing all this to isolate you from your loved ones emotionally. At some point, you might start to feel trapped in the relationship, without a way out.

If you have lost touch with your friends, family

members, and others you depended on in your times of need, you have nowhere to turn when things become too much. When the center of your universe keeps doling out abuse, it becomes hard not to feel emotionally overwhelmed. The narcissist usually thrives in such situations. It helps form an unhealthy dependency on him, which perpetuates the cycle of abuse.

REALITY CHECK

Consider the following checklist. Do you recognize any of these behaviors? If you notice any of these things happening in your relationship, it may be a sign you are in a relationship with a narcissist

- He criticizes the qualities he used to praise you for.
- He criticizes you, not just in private, but in public too.
- He blames you whenever things go wrong, but takes credit for all the good things in the relationship.
- He doesn't hesitate to put you down and never misses an opportunity to make you feel bad about yourself.
- He continually exaggerates your faults while praising himself.

- He talks to you condescendingly.
- When you point out his faults, he conveniently shifts the blame back onto you.
- He does things that make you question your sanity.
- You feel emotionally overwhelmed and isolated from your friends and family.
- He displays extreme mood swings.
- He is never available when you need him.
- If you confront him about anything, he makes you feel clingy and needy.
- He keeps pushing your boundaries, even when you are clearly uncomfortable.
- He seems to have all the control and is the only one with power in the relationship.

6

THE DISCARD STAGE

B e prepared.

Utter and complete disbelief, gut-wrenching shock, and extreme confusion are just some of the many emotions you might experience during the discard stage.

One day everything is going well, and the next, he is gone. The person that you thought was your soulmate is gone. Things may have been hard lately, but you never expected this. He refuses to speak to you, and there is no explanation given. He is just simply not around anymore.

You carefully dissect the relationship and start examining it from every angle; after all, he did say he loved you. But now he refuses to acknowledge your existence. He said he adored you, but now it appears he doesn't need you. When he does finally appear again, he speaks harshly and criticizes everything about you. He generously gave to you out of his own free will, but now he says that you are spoiled. He might even start demanding that you return everything he once gave you.

It once seemed that he couldn't live without you, but now it's over, and you didn't see it coming. Perhaps the most challenging aspect of getting over a narcissistic relationship is the lack of closure. Combine that with pain and confusion, and it can easily overwhelm you.

Let's look at what happens in the third phase of a narcissistic relationship, where the narcissist appears to discard you. You might or might not get to experience this phase, depending on how soon you realize you are dating a narcissist. If you take action before it gets this far, all well and good, but if not, be prepared for heartbreak.

When it happens, there will be plenty of questions running through your mind, with few answers readily available. You are left asking, "Where did he go?" "Why did he leave?" and "Will he come back?"

WHERE DID HE GO?

Where did he go? He is not around anymore; he seems to have abandoned you.

Your presence in his life was to validate him, but he doesn't need that from you anymore, so he pulls away from you for no apparent reason. This might happen suddenly or over a short period of time; but it will be obvious that he is no longer around.

This is confusing to you, because one minute, you are everything to him, the next minute, you are "dropped." One minute he is there, the next he is gone. You feel like he has abandoned you, out of the blue.

There was no explanation given, no discussion about being unhappy and wanting to end the relationship. Sure, things might have been a bit tense lately, and he was being even more critical and abusive than before; but that was still being balanced out to some extent by his good mood days. As far as you were concerned, you were still very much a couple.

WHY DID HE LEAVE?

"Why did he leave?" "Doesn't' he love me?" – you are left asking so many questions. It is incredibly confusing. After all, he needed you one minute, and the next, it was like you meant nothing to him. "Did I hurt him?" Did I say something that pushed him away?" He gives you no reasons, and you are left scratching your head.

The truth is that even if you loved *him*, it was never real love from his side. He never actually loved you; you merely served a purpose. You were a source of supply that catered to his need. Your presence in his life was purely to validate him. Since you no longer serve this function well for him, he has no reason to be around you.

The main reason he pulls away so suddenly is that he no longer sees you as a reliable or necessary source of validation in his life. Even if he meant the world to you, you were merely a means to an end for him. But as soon as you no longer met his ego-driven needs, he moved on.

If you had criticized him in any way, he might feel like punishing you. The emotional pain that he causes you by abandoning you actually validates him even more because he sees how much not having him around affects you. That tells him he must be really special. He may even enjoy seeing you suffer.

Most often that not, he will have found someone else. He has discarded you just like a child tossing an old toy to one side when a shiny new one turns up. He now has someone else to "massage-his-ego" and give him the validation he craves, someone that he sees as a better source of supply.

When you look at it objectively, you will realize that the reasons he has gone are:

- You no longer meet his needs or demands.
- You no longer stroke his ego.
- You started understanding when he was manipulating you and started saying no.
- You started to stand your ground and told him when he was wrong.
- You set some boundaries and refuse to compromise them.
- He could no longer bribe you using money or gifts.
- You figured out his lies and confronted him.
- You refused to allow him to keep abusing you.
- You probably told him he is a narcissist.
- You have served your purpose, and he doesn't need you anymore.
- He has found someone else to meet his needs.

WILL HE COME BACK?

The narcissist might be gone forever, or he might come back after a while. To be honest, it would be better for your sake that he never came back into your life. But even if he does return, it will be short-lived. It will only be because he needs a quick-fix ego top-up, and he hasn't yet found a consistent enough supply to replace you.

Sometimes this may become a cycle of leaving and returning, but only if you keep allowing him back into your life. Letting him come back is only delaying the inevitable and prolonging your pain. Ideally, you need to prepare yourself to cut off all ties with him and move on.

Staying in an on-and-off relationship with a narcissist is not healthy for you. If you want to heal yourself, you need a fresh start. The narcissist feeds off of the pain that this causes you, because it makes him still feel important, and keeps him in control. So the best thing you can do in such a situation is to distance yourself. If he does keep coming back, the cycle will end only when you decide that *you* have had enough, and *you* make the decision to move on.

PART 3: HOW IT ENDS

Eventually, all things come to an end.

You may have started out thinking you had the perfect relationship with the perfect partner. But as it played out, you realized this guy was not who you initially thought he was.

As a relationship with a narcissist progresses, you will come to realize things are not what they seem, and the relationship is not going where you had hoped. As you start to discover your partner's true nature, you also start to discover things about yourself and your own behavior that you had never seen before.

7

THE BEGINNING OF THE END

At some point, the victim comes to a realization about the true nature of the relationship. The penny finally drops for her, and she starts to accept that this is going nowhere. This awareness can come as a shock because she has spent so much time and energy trying to make it work, always believing that there was a future. But now she finally realizes that all her effort has been in vain. It dawns on her that the guy she is dating is actually a Narcissist.

As she examines the relationship, she realizes also that the problem with this relationship has been two-fold. The obvious issue is with the narcissistic partner himself. She realizes that he alone is reponsible for that. But she sees that there is another, not-so-obvious factor, which has also contributed to the problem: that is, her own behavior and willingness to have let it happen.

HIM-REALIZATION

As the relationship starts to unravel, you might start wondering about how genuine your partner's feelings really are. You might start to doubt whether he does actually love you at all? You start to realize that he doesn't really care for you, it is all just talk. It dawns on you that he is a manipulator who is taking advantage of you. You start to re-examine all his behavior n your mind, and start to wonder whether he might be a Narcissist.

Here are some typical behaviors you should look out for to confirm your doubts about whether your partner might be a narcissist.

Constant Interruptions

Most of us love to talk, but we also love to listen. However, a narcissist is a poor listener. He will continually interrupt others while they are talking. Take a moment and think about how your regular conversations progress. Does your partner allow you to carry on a conversation without any interruptions? Do you ever get to speak your mind? Does he keep interrupting you whenever you try to say something? Were there any instances where you were sharing some vital information while your partner decided to interrupt the conversation to shift the attention back to him? Perhaps you were telling him about your day at work, and he interrupted you to tell an insignificant instance from his day (maybe he was offered a cup of coffee by his intern).

Hogs Conversations

A narcissist is never happy unless he is the center of attention. Therefore, unsurprisingly, he tries to hog every conversation. If the conversation isn't about him or if he is not the one talking, he is not interested. Narcissists love to talk about themselves, their abilities, and their achievements. While doing this, they don't hesitate to exaggerate their accomplishments.

Narcissists tend to do this because it enables them to feel superior, better, and smarter than anyone else around them. It allows them to feel self-assured. If you notice that your partner constantly hogs the conversations, or always shifts the focus back to him, give yourself some time to consider the likelihood of him being a narcissist.

False Self

Most narcissists love doing things merely to impress others while making themselves seem good. They have a trophy complex that manifests itself in different aspects of their life. A narcissist uses people, status, accomplishments, or even objects to represent his true self, whereby he substitutes his real self with a false self.

Does your partner love glorifying his accomplishments, regardless of how insignificant they might be? Does it ever feel like he is exaggerating his talents or skills? Does it feel like he is continually saying or doing things merely to impress others? If yes, then your partner has narcissistic tendencies.

No Boundaries

A narcissist has no regard for the feelings, thoughts, or even possessions of others. The idea of personal boundaries doesn't exist in his mind. So constantly oversteps and intrudes on the boundaries others have. He might also use others without any sensitivity or consideration. For instance, your partner might be borrowing your items or money without ever really returning it. Does he constantly break his promises? Does he fail to deliver on all his commitments? Does he show any remorse when he doesn't keep up his promises? Take some time and carefully consider these questions. For example, if he didn't show up for dinner as he promised, does he apologize? Or does he say something along the lines of, "It's your fault because you didn't remind me?"

No Empathy

Lack of empathy is the inability to feel how another person is feeling. It's one of the essential characteristics of a narcissist. They are unable to make others feel validated, understood, accepted, or heard. How does your partner react when you tell him you had a bad day at work? Does he seem caring if you tell him you fought with your best friend? Does he get bored whenever you start expressing certain things that make you feel bad or sad? His inability to sympathize or empathize with others is a sign of his narcissism.

Friend Circle

Narcissists don't have a large circle of friends. Even if they do, they don't really have any long-term or real friends. Narcissists spend a lot of their time putting on a face to present to the world. So, it becomes incredibly difficult for them to have any real friends that truly know them.

Empathy is essential for forming relationships. Their lack of empathy prevents them from being able to form meaningful two-way relationships. If you think about it, you will realize that your partner has only casual acquaintances, no life-long close friends. But he has plenty of nemeses, and other people he trash-talks. So, what do you think about your partner's friend circle? If you are having any doubts about your partner's personality, then it's a good idea to look at the company he keeps.

Picks on You

At first, it might sound like he's teasing you playfully. However, this teasing gradually escalates and starts becoming more constant and mean. It reaches a point where he starts criticizing everything you do. From the clothes you wear, to the people you meet, or even the way you walk. Anything and everything you do will be met with criticism. Name-calling, taunts, mean jokes, and hurtful jabs are how a narcissist tries to put you down. Does it feel like your partner criticizes everything you do? Do you ever receive any praise? Try to answer this question honestly, and you will have your answer.

Always Right

You can never win an argument with a narcissist. Since narcissists consider themselves to be superior to others, they also believe that they know it all and are always right about everything. You cannot debate or compromise with a narcissist since he believes he is always right. A narcissist might not even view disagreements as disagreements. Instead, he merely thinks of them as an opportunity to teach you something new.

If you find that your partner doesn't hear you, cannot understand you, doesn't accept responsibility for his mistakes, and doesn't try to compromise – he is probably a narcissist.

Doesn't Care

Does it ever feel like everything in your relationship is about him? Is everything designed to fit his needs and requirements? In a healthy relationship, both partners should equally contribute to the growth of the relationship. However, if it feels like you're the only one doing everything, while your partner merely takes credit for all the good things, then it's time to reconsider your relationship. If you have a nagging feeling that he doesn't care about you the way he claims to, then listen to your gut. Don't ignore your intuition. If it seems like he doesn't care, it's because he doesn't care. So should you care about him?

Realizing that you are dating a narcissist can come as a shock. After all, you had spent so much time investing in the relationship, thinking it was the real deal. That realization can make you start to question yourself and wonder what on earth you were thinking?

SELF-REALIZATION

As you begin to realize the true nature of your partner's character, you will also start to see yourself more clearly, too. As it dawns on you that he is a narcissist, it may also dawn on that you have been letting him get away with it.

Please don't misunderstand me; I am not saying that you are to blame for being abused. The narcissist is quite clearly responsible for all the hurt and abuse you have had to endure. But the truth is that no one can get away with treating you poorly unless you allow them to. So in some ways, by allowing it to happen, you have been complicit in perpetuating the narcissistic abuse.

It's time to realize that you have the power to prevent others from exploiting you. You don't have to look for ways to validate him or his behaviors. You should realize that you have essentially allowed yourself not to count in this relationship and have instead made it all about him and his wants.

Your inability to set clear boundaries is a significant reason why your partner managed to get away with his abuse. You might have allowed many things without even realizing it, but you shouldn't blame yourself or believe you deserved to endure the trauma of such a toxic relationship.

What we are talking about here is pure self-realization. By understanding "who" you have been in this relationship, you can take steps to protect yourself from similar situations in the future.

How was I complicit?

Unknowingly, you might have been perpetuating your narcissistic partner's agenda even when he wasn't around. For example, since a narcissist has extreme views of perfection, which are humanly impossible to attain, it's natural that any partner he is with will fall short of his unrealistic standards.

The narcissist then continually points out your flaws, and even though you are not, you start believing that you are flawed. The faults he points out may not be real, but hearing it from him regularly, conditions you to accept it as true. (We all start believing certain things if they are told to us repeatedly.)

So you end up following through with his attempts at "fixing you." You start lecturing and berating yourself if you do something that is deemed unacceptable to him. Instead of realizing that he has set impossibly high standards of perfection, you start looking for ways to make him see that you are perfect.

But why would an intelligent and rational person do this? If you stop to think about it, this doesn't make any sense. But he has you thinking that you are the problem and that by changing yourself to meet his standards, you will fix the relationship.

The more criticism you receive, the greater your desire becomes to achieve perfection. In a bid to please your narcissistic partner, you forget about yourself. Gradually you lose all sense of self and self-worth. Because you are trying to please him, you go to great lengths to do everything he wants you to do. You even do things that are not in sync with your values, beliefs, or comfort level. Unless you understand the basic flaw in your thinking, you will continue in a cycle of narcissistic abuse. If you want to move on from a toxic relationship and heal yourself, then self-realization is essential.

Often, individuals in toxic relationships with a controlling partner such as a narcissist, display certain traits of codependency. This is not always the case, but if you are looking at yourself, trying to work out how you got into this mess, codependency is one issue that is worth considering.

CODEPENDENCY

Codependency is the "enabling" behavior of someone in a close relationship with a person who has an addictive or driven behavior. Rather than challenging them, the codependent responds to the subject in such a way that allows them to continue operating in that unhealthy behavior or addiction. It's as if the codependent partner is giving them permission to continue doing it.

Codependency is not an inherent behavior; it's a way of operating that most of us learn from others, usually from our parents or primary caregivers in childhood. When we are children, we watch, learn, and observe our parents and their actions. Maybe your mother, father, or a primary caregiver had issues with boundaries, was always the martyr, could never say no to others, or couldn't communicate their desires effectively. You will have learned from watching them, and unwittingly accepted that as a proper way to behave. Then, as an adult, you take all that with you into your intimate relationships.

Children who grow up in a household where the parents are emotionally unavailable are at a higher risk of becoming codependent later in life. They are often drawn to people who are emotionally unavailable and end up in relationships with them. Not knowing how to put their foot down and end such relationships, they stay in them for longer than they should, holding out hope that their partner may yet change. They believe that if they just manage to hang in there for a little while longer, provide more love and support, and be more understanding of their partner's needs, they would finally experience love from them.

One consequence of becoming codependent is that you don't establish healthy boundaries to protect yourself from emotional or physical harm. Indeed, it should be a warning sign to your partner if you are willing to endure abuse from him. But instead, your partner starts realizing he can get away with acting selfishly or abusively, simply because you don't object to it.

At the core of this is a clear lack of awareness of what is going on in your life. You keep getting into loveless relationships because you have never clearly under-stood what a good partnership should look like.

Codependents often endure mental, physical, emotional, or even sexual abuse that is dished out by their partners. And yet they hang around because they believe their partner can change. They believe that by enduring his behavior, they will finally receive the love they want from him.

Codependent individuals often look for external sources that will enable them to feel better about them-selves. They end up in relationships that are unhealthy, and instead of realizing that, they'll look for ways in which they can "fix" their partner. They don't believe they deserve love, so they end up settling for so much less.

The following traits are often displayed by those who are codependent:

You Put the Needs of Others Before Your Own

A codependent individual has an inherent tendency to place the needs of others before their own happiness. It's okay to think about others before yourself, occasionally. But, you cannot be utterly selfless in all aspects of your life. If you find that you continually go out of your way to do things for others, it's a sign you may be codependent. It is indeed a characteristic that a narcissist can easily exploit.

You Feel You Are Responsible for Their Happiness

You feel responsible for the happiness of others around you, but also, in some ways, you feel accountable for their actions too. So, you end up doing more than your fair share to maintain the peace in a relationship.

You Make Excuses for Them

Do you always make excuses for your partner? Do you try to cover up his faults or mistakes? Do you keep coming up with reasons to justify all his actions? If your partner is regularly critical of you, instead of understanding that you are in a toxic relationship, you start internalizing the criticism. You come up with explanations to justify his unfair treatment, and you start believing the criticism, thinking you are flawed and inadequate.

You Are Scared of Being Alone

Are you scared that you will end up being alone? Are you worried you will never find someone who will love you unconditionally, or concerned that all your relationships will end in heartbreak? Most of us tend to worry about these things from time to time, but a codependent can feel frightened by the idea of being alone. Since their happiness and everything stems from an external source, they know they cannot be truly happy just by themselves.

Do you identify yourself in any of the traits mentioned above? I admit that I certainly did. Once you recognize your codependency, it improves your overall self-awareness. As you understand what codependency is, you can start to make the changes required to break free from any unhealthy relationship patterns you might be following. Understanding and accepting who you are is an essential first step in making any changes.

8

WHO AM I?

It's time to take a firm stand for yourself and start untangling this complicated relationship with your narcissistic partner. It's time you start remembering who you really are. Who were you as a child? Who were you before you met this guy? What were your hopes and dreams when you were growing up? Are they reflected in how you are living now? As you get back in touch with who you really are, it becomes easier to start separating yourself from the relationship. It becomes easier to be aware of and recognize that the behavior you are tolerating, is abuse. And it becomes easier to break free of it.

HOW TO STOP CODEPENDENT BEHAVIOR

So, once you recognize you have been displaying codependent behavior, how do you go about trying to change?

Start Untangling

Codependents have a natural tendency to want to control and rescue others, so they end-up getting entangled in problems that aren't their own. But that tendency prevents them from being able to form relationships that are healthy and balanced.

Since codependents love to hang around those they can help in one way or another, narcissists love to hang around them. As a codependent, your urge to help others works in favor of the narcissist since he loves being the center of attention and recognizes you as someone who you will willingly attend to him. Your diminished sense of "self" makes it hard for you to distinguish where your desires stop and where his desires begin.

His needs are not your needs. What you see as being kind to him is not always the case. Just because he has a demand does not mean that you are supposed to fulfill it. Yes, it's good to be aware of the needs of these around us, but you are not obliged to satisfy them. Therefore, it's time to start untangling his needs and wants, from your own.

Becoming more aware of your own desires and being able to see them as separate from his, is essential in starting to regain your sense of yourself, and regain control of your life.

Understand Yourself

You are a complicated individual, just like the rest of us. You don't have to allow your roles in life to define you. You don't have to let others define you. You are the only one with the power to decide who you are. Getting to know yourself is not selfish. Making yourself your priority is not wrong, and is especially desirable while you work on healing yourself. Here are some simple questions you can ask yourself:

- What do I like to do for fun?
- How do I want others to treat me?
- What are my beliefs?
- What are my goals in life?

Self-Reflection

While dissecting your narcissistic relationship, you

must pay heed to the part you played in it. If you are codependent, it can be tricky to see yourself and the relationship objectively. You may even deny that you have any codependent tendencies. Denial is a simple self-protection mechanism that your mind uses to shield itself from unpleasant truths. Unless you acknowledge that your complicity was your undoing, you will end up making the same mistakes again in the future.

So, think about all the little ways you enabled the narcissist to carry on in his abusive manner. Perhaps you have a tough time saying no, or maybe you find it hard to confront anyone if they hurt you. Once you understand and accept any such inclinations you have, you can change yourself for the better.

Loving Yourself

You must learn to love yourself the way you are. You don't have to go out of your way or put yourself in harm's way to make others like you. Codependency stems from feelings of worthlessness, insecurity, and a belief that you are unlovable. All these feelings are not only misplaced, but they are downright wrong. It's okay to doubt yourself once in a while since it provides scope for self-reflection. But if you don't love yourself and give yourself what you need, you will end up trying to appease others and please them at your expense. If you keep doing this, it will get harder and harder for you to form any healthy or meaningful relationships in your life.

FINDING YOURSELF

A relationship with a narcissist is bound to make you forget about yourself. Since a narcissistic relationship only caters to the needs of the narcissist, you might lose yourself along the way while trying to meet all his demands. The focal point of the relationship becomes the narcissist's ego and making sure he is satisfied. Therefore, if you want to move away from such a relationship, and start healing yourself, it's time to put the focus back onto you.

Somewhere along the way, you lost sight of yourself and who you really are. Its time to start finding yourself again and reacquaint yourself with the true "you."

Who Am I?

It's time that you rethink and re-establish who you are, and what your fundamental values are. Spend some time and think about all that you desire from a relationship. Most of us like the idea of finding a partner and being in love, but few us are aware of what we truly want from a relationship. If you have no clarity about what your desires are, it becomes incredibly easy for others to manipulate you.

When you know what you like, it becomes easier to stand your ground and protect your values and beliefs. It's quite likely that you might have been ignoring your values and beliefs during the narcissistic relationship. When you know who you are, you make better decisions. If you don't become aware of who you are, you are bound to repeat the same mistakes.

Sometimes, all you need to re-establish your beliefs and values is just to remind yourself of what they are. Narcissists and other emotional predators can make you question every thought or belief you have. So what do you believe about life? What do you believe about how things should be? How do you expect to be treated?

What Do I like?

In a relationship with a narcissist, you spend a lot of time doing what *he* wants. You watch the movies that *he* likes. You go to the restaurants that *he* loves. You spend time at weekends engaged in the pursuits that give *him* fulfillment. But what about you? What things do *you* like? Do you know? It may have been a long time since you even thought about it? You may be totally out of touch with yourself.

So you need to ask yourself some questions. Grab a notepad and pen and sit down and ask yourself: If your partner wasn't the one choosing, what movies would you watch? What restaurants would you eat at? How would you spend your time at the weekends? What music would you choose to listen to? Where would you choose to go on vacation?

Going through an exercise like this can be quite tricky, especially when you have spent so much time letting someone else's likes and dislikes influence you. It may take a little while for you to rediscover yourself deep down in the recesses of your neglected true self. It may feel strange to reconnect with the person you used to be. For some, it may be the first time you have ever actually looked at yourself and gained a sense of your self autonomously.

Once you realize what you need and what you like, you can easily compare the current state of your relationship to the ideal you have in your mind. If it feels like the existing relationship falls short, then it's time to make some changes.

. . .

How Do I Want to Be Treated?

Regardless of how the narcissistic relationship might have made you feel, you need to acknowledge that you are the only one who has control of your life. No one else can control you unless you consciously give away that power to others. Therefore, you are the only one who can determine how you get to be treated.

Taking care of yourself must be your priority. No one else can do it for you. So, take some more time, and start making a list of all the things that you cannot tolerate anymore. Down one side of a page, list the ways that your partner oversteps the mark in his interactions with you. How does he talk to you? What language does he use? What is his attitude? How does he touch you? Is he respectful of you?

On the other side of the page, list all the ways you would prefer to be treated. Make this list as clear as possible, so that you arm yourself with the knowledge of the treatment you know you deserve. How does what you want, compare to how you are being treated now?

When you have clarity about how you wish to be treated in a relationship, you condition yourself to expect more. You empower yourself to elicit better treatment from those around you. Don't be afraid to demand to be treated well, especially by a romantic partner. It is your basic human right to expect to be treated with respect and kindness, so don't feel any shyness about demanding to be treated like that by those that say they love you. By starting to communicate your expectations now, it will help improve your overall sense of confidence. It will also help prevent you from falling into toxic relationships in the future.

SELF-ACCEPTANCE

Do you like who you are? Is there something about yourself you want to change? Do you like the person you have become? It's a strange truth about the human condition that most of us are quite good at concentrating on our negative qualities and obsessing over them. While at the same time, we seem to lack even a basic ability to see any positive qualities in ourselves.

Self-acceptance, as the name suggests, is our ability to accept ourselves exactly the way we are, without any changes. It's quite easy to love something when it appears perfect in our estimation. But we don't see ourselves as perfect, so we find ourselves hard to love. Every flaw that we see in ourselves is magnified far beyond reality under the microscope of our self-critique. So when you add in a tendency to be codependent, it can make it very difficult for a person to practice self-acceptance.

A narcissist might have conditioned you to believe that unless you are perfect, you don't deserve love. But that's not true. You need to give yourself unconditional love now; and accept yourself just as you are, warts and all.

With self-acceptance comes a sense of happiness, which is internal; no-one else can take it away from you. And since you no longer rely on external sources to make you feel good about yourself, you reduce your susceptibility to emotional manipulation.

Your self-esteem stems from your self-acceptance. Unless you accept yourself, just the way you are, your self-esteem will always suffer. But when do accept yourself and your self-esteem is healthy, you naturally stop compromising your values for the sake of a relationship.

Let's look at simple steps you can follow to kickstart your journey to self-acceptance.

Face Your Fears

We all have certain fears that we keep repressed and suppressed. These fears are often stored away in the deep recess of our minds. Most of us are so scared of the unknown that we always end up sticking to what we know. We think it's better to deal with the devil we know, than the one we don't. Perhaps you are scared that no one will love you or that you aren't deserving of love? The fear of not being loved is one of the reasons why victims of narcissistic abuse prolong an unhealthy relationship, even when they know it's toxic. This kind of thinking keeps them stuck, paralyzed from taking the action they need to improve their life.

FEAR can be better understood by the acronym False Evidence Appearing Real. What we fear is usually an idea rather than a reality. When we confront our fears head-on, we suddenly discover that the things we fear don't actually exist. The fear is just the possibility of what might happen, but when it comes to it, there is nothing there. All the power of fear is in the unanswered tension, which dissipates the moment we face it.

Be Kind

You must learn to be kind to yourself. Being kind to yourself shows that you care about yourself. If you can't be kind to yourself, how can you expect anyone else to be kind to you? Keep in mind that you're the only person who can judge yourself. Regardless of the opinion others may have about you, they have no right to judge you, so why judge yourself? You know that you can be your own worst enemy, so it's time to start practicing some self-kindness and go easy on yourself.

Imperfections

We are all flawed; no one is perfect. Even if your narcissistic partner made you believe that perfection is realistic, it is not. We are imperfect, and that's what makes us human. It's okay to aim toward perfection to improve ourselves, but in doing so, you must take care not to lose sight of who you are and what you really want. Start embracing your imperfections. Don't change yourself because someone else tells you to. Change yourself only for your own good, and do it in a way that suits you.

Positivity

In a narcissistic relationship, you get used to hearing negative criticism. Negativity is destructive: it eats away at your self-confidence and ability to be creative. To counteract that, you need to start surrounding yourself with messages of positivity. Reconnect with people who you lost touch with over the years, people who can speak positively into your life. Start spending time with those who genuinely love you and wish the best for you. When you surround yourself with positivity, those positive emotions are bound to rub off on you. And by merely changing your attitude, it becomes easier to deal with tough or challenging circumstances in life.

Don't Make It Personal

Remember that everyone is entitled to their opinions. Just because someone else thinks something about you, it doesn't make it so. So, stop taking criticism personally. Others' comments rarely reflect the truth, and they tend to say more about them than about us. So don't take anything personally in life. If you keep allowing negative comments made by others to bring you down, it will stunt your emotional and spiritual growth.

Believe in Yourself

You are capable of attaining greatness. You are capable of living a happy and fulfilling life. You don't have to compromise on anything. Start believing in yourself, regardless of what others tell you. If someone tells you that you cannot do something, prove them wrong. You are a strong, independent, and powerful woman. You can deal with all the challenges that life throws your way.

Self-Forgiveness

One issue that victims of narcissistic abuse need to address is self-forgiveness. You need to forgive yourself. Whatever has happened is in the past. The past can't be changed. But, you can learn from it to ensure that you don't make the same mistakes in the future. If you don't forgive yourself, you are holding on to the abuse you endured. You did not ask for it; it is your abuser who is at fault. So stop blaming yourself for what happened to you. Forgive yourself, accept that you endured a traumatic experience, and start dealing with it. Self-forgiveness improves your self-awareness and makes it easier for you to accept yourself the way you are.

GETTING HELP

Overcoming an emotionally abusive situation is never easy. If you have dealt with a narcissist, you really should seek some professional or external help. Emotional abusers or manipulators like narcissists often convince their victims that they are the only ones whose opinion matters and that they are always right. Narcissists believe they know everything and condition their victims to share that belief. Therefore, it's a good idea to seek external help because your experience with the narcissist will have clouded your judgment.

Ideally, it is best to seek professional help from a psychotherapist or a counselor; but if you feel like you aren't ready to take this step yet, at least start talking to *someone*. You need to get the perspective of someone outside of your relationship. A close friend or family member is an excellent place to start, You need to talk to someone who has your best interests at heart, will push you in the right direction, and prompt you to take the right action to help yourself. Don't allow your pride to get in the way and prevent you from asking for help. You are not doing yourself a favor by refusing to get help. It's okay to ask for help, and if you think you need to talk to someone, you are right!.

9

DRAWING THE LINE IN THE SAND

In any relationship, there are two people; and each of those people has their own identity. Each should know who they are, separate from the other. Knowing where you start and where your partner ends is crucial in establishing a vibrant, healthy relationship. It makes for healthy interactions and enables you to be able to relate with each other appropriately.

Establishing physical and emotional boundaries is essential in all aspects of life, and relationships are no exception. Every machine built by mankind has a limit, and when pushed beyond that limit, it stops functioning. Likewise, as humans, we all have limits. Unless we acknowledge and respect our limits and set boundaries around them, others will get away with pretty much anything they want. So let's look at what boundaries are and how to establish and maintain them.

BOUNDARIES

Boundaries. What are they? When I first heard the phrase "setting boundaries for yourself," I genuinely did not understand what it meant. I had grown up with no understanding of my personal power. I had no idea that I had the right to dictate what happened to me; no concept that I was able to choose how I wanted to be treated. I just believed that I had to do what anyone else told me.

When I was a child at primary school, others picked up on this and realized they could tell me to do anything, and I would do it. So one day, in the playground, the bossiest child in our group told me to lie on the ground so that they could all walk on me. I had no understanding that I could say no, and so I did it. I literally laid down and let others walk over my back. What a metaphor!

Looking back, I find it incredible to think that I was like that. I have changed so much since then that I hardly even recognize myself in that memory. What happened that day I should never have allowed. Any child with a healthy ego would not have done that. It was quite a scarring experience that helped weaken my sense of self so much that I spent many years of my life with a self-belief that said: "I do not matter." I really did not believe that I had the right to choose anything, especially not how others could relate to me.

It crossed over into other areas of my life too. As I advanced through my teenage years and into early adulthood, I thought that others could have things, but not me. Others could have money or overseas holidays or expensive things, but that didn't apply to me. I really was quite a pitiful figure when I think about it. It took a lot of emotional healing and personal growth to become who I am today.

Boundaries are how you describe yourself, how you define yourself relative to the world around you. They are how you state to the world that: I am this, but not that; I like this, but not that; I will do this, but not that. They are an essential part of a human being's make-up.

To know your boundaries is to know yourself. No-one else can tell you how to think or feel in any given situation. We are all unique and have our way of experiencing the world around us. You are allowed to say

"Yes," and you are allowed to say "No." You are entitled to be "you" and define yourself as you truly are.

To establish a healthy boundary, you first need to know and understand your limits. You can't set a limit if you can't name it. If you don't know where you stand, you can't set a boundary around it.

Therefore, take some time for self-reflection and come up with your physical, mental, emotional, and spiritual limits. Think about all the things you can tolerate and accept. Think about what makes you happy and relaxed, and contrast that with what makes you feel stressed or uncomfortable.

When you find the spot where you start to feel stressed or uncomfortable, it shows you that you have passed your limit, so you know to set your boundary to just before that point.

The most common boundaries we all to need to set are:

- Emotional boundaries - you are allowed to feel the way you do in any given situation.
- Physical boundaries - your personal space matters regardless of what others tell you.
- Intellectual boundaries - you have the right to entertain your thoughts and opinions.
- Social boundaries - you have the right to

choose your friends and pursue your preferred social activities.

- Spiritual boundaries - you have the right to set your own spiritual beliefs.

Learn to tune in to your feelings while establishing boundaries. There are two cues you must pay attention to, and they are discomfort and resentment. Whenever you notice either of these feelings, rate them on a scale of one to 10. If a specific interaction or situation causes noticeable resentment or discomfort, it means you are crossing one of your boundaries. Take a moment and ask yourself, "Why am I feeling like this?" Once you answer this, move onto the next question, "Is there something about this interaction or the other person's expectations that is bothering me?"

Resentment stems from the feeling of being unappreciated or taken advantage of. Discomfort comes from feeling that you are asking yourself to go beyond what you consider to be okay. Whenever you notice these emotions, it's a sign that you are pushing yourself beyond your limits; either because you feel guilty from a choice you have made, or because someone is imposing their expectations or values on you.

Have you ever felt uncomfortable doing something that your partner asked? Did you feel like he was pushing you to do something you didn't want to do? If so, then you were violating your boundaries. Tuning into your emotions is vital in getting to set healthy boundaries.

How have you let your boundaries be crossed in the past?

As you go about redefining your personal limits, take some time to consider how you may have let your boundaries be crossed in the past.

What was your childhood like?

What role did you play in your childhood? If you had narcissistic parents or codependent parents, then you might have played the role of a caretaker. Such child-hood conditioning makes you focus on the needs of others and allows yourself to get drained physically and emotionally, so you might be used to placing the needs of others before your own needs. Have you since been "serving" your partner in the same way? Remember that a narcissistic partner might be exploiting the conditioning you received as a child.

What is your current relationship with your partner like?

Keep in mind that a healthy relationship is supposed to be reciprocal. There should be a balance between "give" and "take" in any relationship. If the balance is not there, it may be a sign that you are allowing your boundaries to be violated. Have there been times when your partner made you feel guilty for not placing his needs before your own? Do you feel guilty if you try and do something for yourself?

You are your first priority

Start prioritizing yourself. It's not a selfish thing to do; it's a responsible stance to take that empowers you to be able to look after others. You must take care of yourself before you can think about helping anyone else. It's one of the reasons why, on an airplane, you are told to put your oxygen mask on first before helping others. What help can you be to anyone else if you cannot help yourself? So, start thinking about yourself.

Always remind yourself that you deserve to be taken care of. As a child, your parents had the responsibility of taking care of you. But as an adult, the one person who is responsible for taking care of you is YOU! You are your own caregiver now, and the first step in taking care of yourself is to set healthy boundaries. That will help you to address any of the toxic behaviors your narcissistic partner exhibits, and allow you to enjoy better interactions while protecting your mental and emotional well-being.

MARKING YOUR TERRITORY

Once you know what your boundaries are, it is time to establish them. Just like a land-owner putting up fences around his property, you also need to take action that tells the world where those boundaries are. It can be daunting, but having gone through the exercise of finding out who you are and what you want, you will have developed a new confidence and found strengths that you don't even know about yet.

Be Assertive

Once you know your boundaries, it becomes easier to understand what your expectations are. By identifying where the line is, you are automatically telling yourself what kind of behaviors you can and cannot tolerate.

So the next time your narcissistic partner treats you in a way that does not sit well with you, you can assert your new position. For example, one boundary you may have set for yourself is that you will no longer allow your partner to criticize you. So, the next time he does so, you can inform him that you are no longer prepared to accept the criticism he is making. Don't state your boundary like it's a request. It's not a request; it is your right. It's an inalienable right that he cannot take it away from you.

You don't have to state all your boundaries in one go. You don't want to read out your list as a new set of rules that need to be obeyed. Firstly that would be very confrontational to a narcissist, and secondly, he would probably just laugh and dismiss you. That is not the reaction you want to get, and one that you probably won't be ready to deal with yet anyway. So ideally, you want to establish your new boundaries one at a time, as and when the appropriate situations arise. There is no rush. And you will gain confidence each time you assert yourself in this way.

Set Consequences

When you establish your boundaries, you must also set consequences for what will happen if each boundary is violated. Remember that land-owner? He will have put up signs on his fences, saying, "Trespassers will be prosecuted." Those signs are stating the consequence for anyone daring to cross his boundaries. Likewise, you also need to state clearly what will happen if your partner crosses your new boundaries. You get to decide what those consequences are.

For instance, if he starts to criticize you and your boundary is to not allow him to criticize you, then you can decide that the consequence is that you end the conversation there and then, before it turns into a session of bullying. Or, if you have set a physical boundary to prevent things from going further sexually than you are comfortable with yet, you can set the consequence of physically distancing yourself from him if he tries to go too far. If you are at home, then move away to another room; if you are in a public setting, then just leave from there.

If he refuses to accept your boundaries, you have the power to determine your next move.

THE FREAKOUT

When you first start setting and implementing boundaries while in a narcissistic relationship, be prepared for an unpleasant reaction from your partner. Narcissists love being in control and will hate it when you try to resume control of your life once again. What you are doing is putting your foot down, and saying that you no longer want to tolerate his narcissistic abuse. Since that is not what he is used to, he is likely to react unfavorably. He may freak out and get angry, but don't be discouraged if he does. It is just a sign that you are doing the right thing.

When he gets upset, you have no reason to feel guilty. You are not responsible for his reaction, and don't let him make you think otherwise. Understand that you are responsible only for your own emotions, not anyone else's. You don't have the power to regulate how others feel or act, so don't allow it to discourage you from continuing to uphold your new boundaries. You mustn't start to compromise again now that you are acting boldly for the first time in this relationship. If you give in to the guilt or start feeling bad, you just send the wrong signal. He needs to know he is dealing with the "new you."

Be Calm

Narcissists love drama. They especially love causing it. But you can refuse to give him the drama he loves by explaining your boundaries clearly and calmly. Ensure that your explanation doesn't leave any room for discussion. It is not a negotiation; you are not asking for his opinion: you are just informing him of your expectations. You don't have to explain them to him or tell him why. They SIMPLY ARE. If he tries belittling you or forcing you to change your mind, stand your ground. Be confident and hold firm while calmly stating that what you're doing is in your best interest. That should effectively end the conversation.

Be Aware

Narcissists love acquiring information about others. They do this by continually quizzing you about your life. The purpose is to identify your weaknesses, which they then use to criticize you. If you seem a little unsure about anything, he will take it as a sign of weakness and criticize you about it.

For example, your narcissistic partner might start asking what your career plans are. It might seem nice that he cares about you, but he doesn't; his ulterior motive is selfish. Once you start opening up, he will memorize that information and use it to criticize anything you do career-wise.

So be aware that he might start probing you about your new boundaries and why you feel the need to behave "so selfishly." If a question makes you uncomfortable, you don't have to answer it. Don't fall into the trap; try and shift the conversation to something else, or just end the conversation.

STANDING YOUR GROUND

Stay strong and defend your position. Establishing and implementing your boundaries is your absolute right, and no one can take that away from you. Your partner will likely not be finding this comfortable, though. He cannot get away with his old narcissistic ways if you keep defending your position. He might try various strategies to try and get you to relinquish your new-found control. He might become quite aggressive, or he might try the opposite and become extremely friendly, just to try and convince you to let go and surrender.

Keep in mind that he is an expert manipulator and will try everything he possibly can to regain his control over your life. But if you keep giving in to his demands and pressures, you will never be able to do anything for yourself. You have the right to make yourself happy. If your partner truly loved you, he would never do anything to compromise your boundaries. But if he cannot respect your decisions, then it's a clear sign that you are in an unhealthy relationship.

Self-Checks

Make time to check in with yourself regularly. In a narcissistic relationship, the level of self-care that is required is quite high. If your partner's narcissism is wearing you down, consider seeking counseling or other emotional support. Keep in mind that you have the right to live your life peacefully. You have the right to lead a healthy and happy life. You deserve the peace of mind you crave.

Boundaries are essential in every relationship. However, once you start establishing them, and sticking to the consequences when they are crossed, it can be quite mentally and emotionally exhausting. So take time out for yourself.

Also, as you progress, make sure that you regularly reassess the plan to determine if you need to change your boundaries, or add any new ones to your list.

An Escape Plan

Have an escape plan, a way to step out and relieve the pressure. If you feel that any negative interaction is harming your self-worth, you have the right to end it immediately. If one of your boundaries gets violated, or if you start feeling uncomfortable, use your escape plan. It could be something as simple as telling your partner that you need some time away from him. Maybe you can go out for a walk, or visit a friend, or if it's a phone call that is bothering you, end the call. Regardless of what you do, just make sure that the steps you take help you move away from, or out of an unhealthy situation.

There can be severe cases where you might have to temporarily or permanently end the relationship. For instance, if your narcissistic partner is an impulsive liar or has a drug problem, then it's a good idea to stay away from him until he seeks the help he needs. If he does this, take some time, and then consider your next move. You don't owe him anything and don't allow him to tell you otherwise.

MOVING ON

You are not responsible for your partner's reactions or feelings. You can share how you wish him to treat you in the relationship, but you cannot force him to do anything he doesn't want to do. If he cannot accept the changes you have made for yourself, if he cannot respect your decisions and encourage you in them, maybe he is not the right guy for you. You have the right to be treated with fairness, love, and respect. If your partner cannot do this, then perhaps it's time to move on.

DECIDING ON THE FATE OF THE RELATIONSHIP

Relationships are rarely easy. Just like anything worthwhile, a good relationship will always require a certain amount of effort to maintain it. However, being in a relationship with a narcissist requires a whole new level of effort; it's a different ball game altogether, in a league of its own.

A relationship with a narcissist is emotionally draining, and often tense. And you can never really tell what is going to happen next. Even if things seem to be going well, his emotions are like a ticking time-bomb: you can never guess when the narcissist's rage might be triggered. So you spend your life walking around him on egg-shells, carefully trying not to upset him.

Not all narcissists are violent, so the hurt they cause is

not usually physical. But all of them do seem to be devoid of empathy, so most narcissistic abuse is psychological or emotional. And the pain inflicted by mental or emotional abuse is often more lasting. Bruises heal fairly quickly, but emotional wounds last a lot longer.

It might not be a narcissist's intention to hurt their partners, but their driven behavior will always end up hurting them at some point or another. As soon as the narcissist latches onto the strength of his victim, he quickly turns the tables and uses it against them. If you are in a relationship with a narcissist, you must accept that staying with them is a choice to expose yourself to being hurt.

The narcissist will definitely hurt you in some way; if not sooner, then later: but most likely sooner, and often. So there will come a time when you are going to have face a big decision:

…the decision about whether you want the relationship to continue or not?

DO YOU NEED TO END THE RELATIONSHIP?

Now that you have realized you are in a relationship with a narcissist, what do you want to do? You have the power to decide the fate of the relationship. The choice is simple: Stay? ...or Go? Remember that you have complete control of yourself and what you want in life. The decision must be yours and yours alone. Don't allow the narcissist to influence your decision-making. Let's look at some things to consider while deciding the fate of your relationship.

There are three simple questions you can ask yourself to determine whether you want to continue the relationship or not:

Is He Willing to Get the Necessary Help?

Is he prepared to seek some external help like counseling? Narcissism is a personality disorder, and with some professional help, he can learn to control his narcissistic tendencies. If he agrees to this request, then give him a trial period. Step back from him for a bit and see if he is keeping his promise or not. Take a while to see if his efforts are genuine and whether he is actually attending those sessions.

Do You Think He Will Truly Change?

Narcissists are usually unlikely to change. Their character flaws are deep-seated, and it will take a concerted effort on their part to heal their emotional wounds and grow into more rounded human beings. However, if your partner does give you a reason to believe that he will change, and you can see the progress he is making, feel free to give the relationship a second chance. But if you notice that he is regularly slipping into his old habits again, count your losses and move on.

Do You Think He Will Give You Your Space?

You need your personal space, even in an intimate relationship. You need time to process your thoughts and explore your personal interests. Your partner must understand that and respect your boundaries. If you want, you can have a conversation about this with him. If you feel that he really doesn't get it, and you think he is incapable of respecting your boundaries, then it may be time to sever all ties and end the relationship. If he promises to respect your boundaries but then starts subtly violating them on a regular basis, then you should probably end the relationship.

STAYING ON

If you decide to pursue the relationship further, ensure that it's your decision and yours alone. Make sure that the narcissist has not manipulated you once again to get his way. You should only stay if you think he is truly capable of participating in a healthy, balanced, equal partnership.

Letting go of a relationship is incredibly difficult, especially when you love someone. So before you make such a momentous decision, you should ask yourself: (a) whether you truly love him? …and (b) whether he truly loves you? If you realize that codependency is guiding your decision, then perhaps the best thing you can do is walk away.

If you believe that you genuinely do love him, then ask yourself if you can make peace with his narcissism? Even if he does manage to make positive changes, the basic traits of a narcissist never entirely go away. But if you believe your partner will make the necessary effort to learn to regulate and control himself, perhaps you can think about staying in the relationship.

Regardless of what your decision is, I can't emphasize enough that you have the power to choose. You can choose whatever you want to do with your life. If you have established boundaries, as in the previous chapter, you will have given yourself the framework to help you evaluate things clearly. Those boundaries help give you the power to choose. Don't ever feel vulnerable or help-less, even if the situation seems hopeless.

At the end of the day, if there is no hope of recovery, or if you think you have just had enough, then walk away.

NO GOING BACK

If you have decided to end the relationship, it is important to stick to the decision you made. Tell yourself that there are no do-overs and not to look back. Once you have made up your mind, it's time to concentrate on breaking free of the narcissistic relationship.

Here are a few things to consider:

Aftermath

The breakup may feel brutal, like a car crash. But if you are the one that's ending the relationship, then you will have had some time to prepare yourself for the backlash. When you announce your decision, he will get angry. He will try to do everything he possibly can to convince you not to leave him. Be strong. Don't change your mind. Trust yourself and the decision you have made and stand firm. If you waver now, he will realize he still has control over you. Don't budge even when he resorts to threatening you with statements like, "You will never find anyone who loves you as I do," or "You will be lost if I'm not in your life." These are simple manipulative tactics he will use because he doesn't want to relinquish his hold over you.

Once you tell him you are breaking up with him, be prepared for him to start begging, pleading, or even negotiating with you. Be prepared to hear plenty of promises about how he just needs another chance to prove himself and that he will change. But keep in mind that, as a narcissist, he is unlikely to do any of the things he promises. Trust yourself, not him. Stick with your decision: one day you will look back and be so glad that you did.

Break the Trauma Bond

In a narcissistic relationship, a Trauma Bond can be formed between the abuser and the victim as a result of intense, shared emotional experiences. As the relationship progressed, you will have got used to his behavior operating in a cycle. He will have oscillated between periods of verbal abuse and periods of praise and admiration of you.

Experiencing these constant mood swings takes a toll on your emotional health. The stress and grief you experience during the abuse phase are balanced-out by the elevated highs you feel when he rewards your good behavior. The cycle becomes addictive.

As a victim, you might not have realized what he was doing, but his manipulative technique of showering you with intermittent love, trapped you into a pattern. It was basically a behavior reward program. However much he abused you, you kept hanging in there because he had conditioned you to expect some praise from him afterward as the cycle tracked back again. So, now that you are incurring his wrath again, albeit on your own terms this time, your emotional memory is expecting to experience the pleasure that usually follows.

You need to be aware of this pattern and not let yourself get dragged back into pleasing him again. You need to wean yourself off the good feeling that you are addicted to experiencing whenever he would turn the charm back on. In other words: Don't let the breakup lead you straight back into a "make-up."

No Contact

Once you have decided to end the relationship, there is a straightforward ground rule you must set for yourself, and that is: "no contact!"

Since a narcissist is a manipulator, you need to guard yourself against giving him any chance to manipulate his way back into your life. It might sound relatively easy, but it takes a lot of willpower and strength to follow through on this promise to yourself.

No contact means *exactly* what it says: No Contact!

It means you are supposed to wipe away all traces of contact with your narcissistic partner from your life. It means blocking his number, deleting him from your social media accounts and avoid meeting or interacting with him at all costs. If you give the narcissist the slightest chance, he will quickly get his claws back into you, and you will be back to where you started.

If you cannot entirely distance the narcissist from your life, then try to separate yourself from him as much as you possibly can. For instance, if your narcissistic partner happens to be your co-worker, then you obviously cannot ignore or avoid him. However, when he's in the same room as you, you can distract yourself with something else. Pay no attention to him, and he will quickly move away.

Gray Rock Technique

If you cannot avoid interacting with the narcissist or meeting him often, you can use a simple technique known as the Gray Rock method.

When you look down at the ground, what do you see? You probably just see grass, rocks, and dirt. Nothing, in particular, stands out, nothing is remarkable. Every gray stone looks just like the other.

Remember that a narcissist is attracted to individuals who are talented, empathetic, creative, or excel in some aspect of their life. So, if you make yourself seem boring, unremarkable, or non-reactive, the narcissist will soon lose interest in you. You merely need to make yourself as unremarkable as a gray rock. A narcissist thrives on attention and reactions from others. If you don't give him the response he's looking for, he will simply get bored and move on.

Mutual Connections

Another simple tactic you can use to disentangle your life from his is to temporarily disassociate yourself from any mutual connections the two of you have. Since a narcissist is such a skilled manipulator, he will undoubtedly try to worm his way back into your life in any way he can. He will not hesitate to use others as leverage to make his way back into your life.

Note that I am not advocating that you stop associating with your friends and family. You don't want to isolate yourself from your support network and those who can help you in your recovery. But, if you have any mutual connections on social media, you might want to remove them from your list.

I know this might sound a little drastic, and a lot of the time will not be necessary. But if the two of you had mutual friends, especially friends that may be closer to him than to you, it may be something that you need to consider. He may try and contact you indirectly through friends' posts or messages that he thinks you will see.

Firstly, you don't want to get dragged into a conversation with him; and secondly, if he knows he cannot win you back, he may engage in character assassination, and start spreading lies and untruths about you, hoping that you will see them and react. The best way to avoid this is not to be able to see any such posts in the first place.

Grieving

Even if it was a bad relationship, it's natural that you will grieve its passing. It's okay to feel the hurt and mourn the loss of your relationship. So give yourself the time and permission to do so. Take all the time you need, and don't let anyone tell you to "stop moping around." You cannot heal yourself unless you process through your emotions. So even if the emotion is grief, accept it, and allow yourself to feel it. It is only by allowing yourself to feel-what-you-feel, that it becomes easier to move on.

REMIND YOURSELF YOUR REASONS

Ending any kind of romantic relationship is a significant change in anyone's life, and escaping a narcissistic relationship is no exception. After the relationship ends, there will be times when you feel down and low.

Experiencing those negative emotions might make you question your decision. You start thinking about all the good times you shared. You start remembering all the compliments he used to give you. You remember the fun things you did together in the early days. And all those positive feelings you experienced start rushing back and tempt you to rekindle the relationship.

We all tend to remember only the good things about a situation and forget the bad things about it because those memories are unpleasant to recall. That causes us to paint a far rosier picture in our minds than what the truth really was. So you will need to remind yourself of what you went through with him. Remind yourself that he was abusive, that he was selfish, and that all the compliments he gave you were part of his manipulative means to gain control of your life.

If the temptation to reconnect with your narcissistic partner starts becoming too much to resist, talk to your loved ones about it. Don't process these thoughts and emotions on your own. Count on your support system to give you the motivation and the willpower to stay true to your decision. You made the right choice.

11

PLANNING A NEW FUTURE

M any victims of narcissistic abuse don't realize that they are victims until quite late in the relationship, or even not until it ends, simply because they don't know what narcissism is, and don't recognize it as abuse. Hopefully, by what you have read so far, you now understand what narcissism is, and what it looks like? You can finally put a name to the pain you experienced and know that you were not going crazy. By gaining this information, you are empowering yourself to avoid getting drawn into that type of situation again.

As you start moving ahead with your life, it's time to leave the nightmare behind and look toward the future. What has happened is now in the past. And an unpleasant relationship experience in the past does not dictate how relationships will be for you in the future. As long as you learn from the experience, you will be able to choose much more successful and enjoyable relationships in the future. You don't have to allow the bad experience you had to determine the course of your life from here on.

WHAT HAPPENS NOW?

Now that you are free, it's time to concentrate on yourself for a while. Here are a few things you can do to help yourself.

Give yourself time

Give yourself some room to breathe. You may need to take a break from relationships for a while. Don't be in a hurry to jump into a new relationship at the first opportunity that comes your way. You don't want to go rushing into anything before you are ready. Just relax.

Your self-esteem might have taken a beating from the abuse you endured, and now that you are free from that, you need to recover. Give yourself the time, space, and opportunity you need to heal and grow. The best way to go about doing that is by practicing self-care and self-love. Look after yourself – get enough sleep, get some exercise. Be patient with yourself. Be kind to yourself. Most of all, go easy on yourself and cut yourself some slack whenever you make a mistake. Remember, you have spent enough time having someone criticize you, so you don't want to start being critical of yourself. Believe in the potential that lies within you and concentrate on your personal development.

Keep Avoiding Him

The game of catch-and-release is quite exciting for a narcissist. So, don't be shocked if you notice that your ex is trying to rekindle the relationship. Use the gray rock technique discussed in the previous chapter while dealing with any interactions with your toxic ex. Narcissists and other emotional vampires thrive on drama and supply. Their only objective is to suck the life out of anyone they can get their hands on. The narcissist may try to keep baiting you, so avoid the bait. Just ignore him if he tries to accuse you of something you neither did nor said. You don't want to get drawn back into defending yourself for something that never happened.

All he is doing is trying to get you to open the door ajar, no matter how slight, so that he can push his way back into your life. If you want to hold onto your sanity, get rid of the narcissist from your life altogether.

No Toxic Friends

Spend some time thinking about your circle of friends,

family members, and those close to you. If you notice any toxicity from any of them, it's probably time to eliminate these relationships. Start weeding out those people who are not 100% on your side. You don't need people like that in your life, especially when you're trying to recover from a negative relationship. There has been plenty of negativity you had to deal with yourself already, and any additional source of it is not welcome at this time. If it feels like someone is holding you back from moving on from the relationship or isn't supportive of you, then stop engaging in conversations with them.

Keep in mind that you are still a little vulnerable and sensitive while you are healing. Therefore, you become easy prey for other toxic individuals. So anyone who is enabling your narcissistic ex in any way is not suitable for you to be around. You certainly don't need to deal with anyone who is sitting on the fence about your toxic relationship. If someone blames you for the trauma, doesn't believe what you experienced, or says they don't want to get in the middle of it, then don't listen to them. You don't need such people in your life at this time; you need friends that will support you and help carry you.

Be prepared that this could mean having to distance yourself from someone dear to you for a while. It might be your closest friend or even a family member. How can you tell when this is a good idea? Well, whenever you interact with anyone, ask yourself how you feel after leaving their presence? Do you feel better or worse? Do you feel safe while talking to them? Or do you feel the need to defend yourself continually?

Someone who is on your side will always have your best interest at heart. If you feel like you always have to defend yourself with a particular person, and feel worse after talking to them, then it's a sign they are someone you should try to avoid. Maybe not forever, but at least for a little while.

LEARNING FROM EXPERIENCE

Learn From the Past

Don't ignore your past. Use everything you went through as a learning experience. Yes, it was painful, but unless you learn from it, you are bound to repeat the same mistakes. Learning from your past takes self-reflection, which can be a tricky thing to do. Reflecting on your past is never easy, but unless you examine how you got to where you are now, it might be hard to move on from here.

It doesn't mean you should start blaming yourself for the abuse you endured. You didn't ask for it, and you didn't deserve it. But that doesn't mean you can't figure out *how* you ended up with someone who ill-treated you and managed to get away with it for as long as they did. When you understand the reason it happened, it becomes easier to ensure that you don't have similar encounters in the future.

You might have to dig deep and go back and look at your childhood. Perhaps certain unaddressed traumatic events scarred you back then. Maybe some childhood abuse that you manage to normalize in your mind is the reason why you had no concept of boundaries? Perhaps you had narcissistic parents who kept reinforcing the idea that you are unworthy of love unless you are perfect? Whatever it was, it led you to end up with a narcissistic partner.

Once you travel into your past and figure out the reasons for how you ended up in the present, you can take corrective action for the future. Life has a funny way of repeating lessons that we refuse to learn, so if you don't want to make the same mistakes again, learn your lessons, forgive yourself, and move on.

Forgive Yourself

Perhaps the hardest part of recovering from narcissistic abuse is to forgive yourself. You may have been conditioned by the narcissist not to like the person you are.

You may be harboring thoughts of shame and blaming yourself for certain mistakes the narcissist convinced you were yours. Now, it's time to let go of that and forgive yourself. You cannot heal if you stay angry with yourself.

The first step here is to determine why you are angry with yourself. Are you upset because you stayed in the relationship for too long? Are you mad because you put up with all the unfair treatment? Are you disappointed with yourself because you feel like you should have known better? Are you upset because you feel like you wasted your time, effort, and life on a person who doesn't deserve it?

Regardless of the reason for your anger, it's time to forgive yourself. A great way to do this is by maintaining a journal. Whenever feelings of anger and negative thoughts come up, start writing them down. Don't hold yourself back; pour your heart out. No-one else will get to read it. Don't judge yourself, whatever you write. Remember, you are just putting your thoughts on a piece of paper.

Once you have written it out, read it back to yourself while imagining that a close friend is saying these things to you. If your best friend came up to you and said, "I'm so upset that I never took a stand for myself, and I stayed for as long as I did with him." What would you say to her? Would you blame her for the abuse she endured? Would you call her stupid for going through that? Or, would you try to reach out and console her? Exactly. Now extend the same compassion towards yourself.

KNOWING YOURSELF, TRUSTING YOURSELF

Regardless of what you do in the future, the one thing you must never do again is compromise on your boundaries. Ensure that all the boundaries you have set stay in place. Review them regularly. Make any changes if necessary, and add new boundaries wherever required.

In the past, you might have ignored your gut and overlooked red flags, even when they were staring you in the face. Now that you are armed with this knowledge of yourself, make the most of it. Whenever you meet someone new, listen to your intuition. Don't become overly suspicious of everyone who comes along, but learn to strike a balance between listening to your gut and using your rational mind.

Once you get practiced at judging people carefully, it becomes easier to stay away from narcissists, manipulators, and other emotional predators.

THE FUTURE OF RELATIONSHIPS FOR YOU

The world is at your feet, and your future is incredibly promising. All that you need to do is maintain a positive outlook, learn your lessons, and don't repeat mistakes. If you notice you are falling into any of your previous patterns, it's time for a self-check. Start taking care of yourself and concentrate on your priorities.

The time you have spent in a narcissistic relationship doesn't determine the course of your future. Yes, you fell in love with a narcissist, and it was not a pleasant experience. However, it doesn't mean everyone you come across will be a narcissist. Most people out there in the world are NOT narcissists!

You *will* meet the right person when the time is right. Keep reminding yourself that you have the right to live a fulfilling life. You deserve to be loved and find someone who loves and appreciates you, just the way you are. You deserve a wonderful, fulfilling relationship with someone that knows you, loves you, and cares for you.

I sincerely believe that you *can,* and you *will* find that!

So don't hold yourself back. Embrace your life. Take control of it today and start expecting to experience the kind of relationship you have always longed for!

AFTERWORD

It's rather unfortunate to have been dating or married to a narcissistic man. There is no upside in a narcissistic relationship. Once the peachy phase of the relationship fades away, it's all downhill from there. The purpose of this book is to equip you with awareness so that you can escape from the abuse you have endured, and help you find your way to freedom and healing.

I hope I have given you enough information to be able to quickly spot a narcissist, and avoid them at all costs. I have described their manipulative tactics and helped you understand what drives them in their abusive behavior. I have shown you how to identify the different stages of a narcissistic relationship, and I have given you advice on how to break free from the cycle of abuse.

It is important to remember that Narcissistic Personality Disorder (NPD) is a psychological condition. The sufferer tends to experience an inflated sense of self and ridiculous ideas of grandeur. A narcissist is selfish, and the only thing that matters to him is his well being. He is incapable of understanding what unconditional love means and cannot truly love anyone else. Individuals often develop NPD because of childhood emotional traumas and then choose victims to conquer based on specific personal traits that they perceive will be most beneficial to their ego.

Every narcissistic relationship goes through three stages. The first stage is all about idealization, then comes the devaluation, and eventually, the narcissist discards their partner. The change in the narcissist's behavior is what defines each stage of the relationship, but at all stages, as he is always exercising control and being manipulative. From believing that you had found your soulmate - to wondering what went wrong, you can feel quite overwhelmed. However, once the relationship with a narcissist ends, you are free to start living without judgment, manipulation, and control.

The narcissist is the fundamental reason why you endured suffering in the relationship; you are not to blame. But getting to understand codependency is a crucial factor in understanding how you ended up in such a situation.

Learning to set and maintain boundaries is vital for everyone, but especially so for someone who has been involved with a narcissist. Getting to know yourself, and understanding what is, and is not acceptable to you, helps you to put boundaries in place so that you can protect yourself from manipulation or emotional attacks. By standing your ground, you can regain control and get your life back on track.

If you want to break free from the relationship, then you have the power and the right to do just that: you are in control of your own life. You don't need to let anyone else tell you what to do.

Recovering from the effects of having been in a relationship with a narcissist can take a while. It is a journey of healing and self-discovery that you need to go on, but one you will never regret. You are stronger than you know.

Different scenarios

In this book, I have concentrated on addressing the situation where a young woman is dating a narcissistic man. That is the scenario I have had the most experience with, and feel I can offer the best advice on. But I am also aware that the roles can be reversed: it can be a young man that finds themself dating a narcissistic woman, though this is much rarer. In such a case, all the same advice applies.

I am also keenly aware that marriages are not exempt from narcissistic abuse. A marriage partner may suffer mistreatment for many years before realizing that the behavior they have endured for so long is actually "abuse." If you are coming to that realization: that you may be married to a narcissist, I strongly advise you to seek professional marriage counseling. You are worth it, and trying to save your marriage is definitely worth the effort.

Finally

As I leave you, the one thing I want you always to remember is that your life can be quite different. Don't be under the misconception that all the men you meet in the future will be narcissists. This is just not the case.

I believe that a beautiful, loving relationship awaits you in the future. Just because you had one bad relationship, it doesn't mean all your relationships will be the same. There is a good man out there waiting for you!

LEAVE A REVIEW

Customer Reviews

⭐⭐⭐⭐⭐ 2
5.0 out of 5 stars ▾

5 star	▓▓▓▓▓▓▓	100%
4 star		0%
3 star		0%
2 star		0%
1 star		0%

Share your thoughts with other customers

Write a customer review ⬅

See all verified purchase reviews ›

I would be incredibly grateful if you could take 60 seconds to leave a quick review on Amazon, even if it's just a few sentences!

>>Click here to leave a quick review

Thank you!

QUICK GUIDE TO SPOTTING A NARCISSIST

(DON'T GET CAUGHT EASILY!)

jenssenbooks.com

Receive your FREE Quick Quiz Checklist to help you:

- Quickly evaluate whether your current partner is a Narcissist?
- Easily spot a Narcissist in the future and avoid getting caught in their trap!

To download your free Quick Quiz Checklist, click:

https://jenssenbooks.activehosted.com/f/1

REFERENCES

4 Phases of a relationship with a narcissist. (2019). Retrieved from https://www.meganholgate.com/2017/05/10/4-phases-of-a-relationship-with-a-narcissist/

Belle, K. (2018). The 7 Startling Phases of Loving a Narcissist. Retrieved from https://psychcentral.com/blog/the-7-startling-phases-of-loving-a-narcissist/

Brown, L. (2019). Breaking up with a narcissist: 12 things you must know. Retrieved from https://hackspirit.com/breaking-up-with-narcissist/

DiBenedetto, C. (2020). 10 Signs You Might Be a Narcissist. Retrieved from https://www.health.com/mind-body/10-signs-you-might-be-a-narcissist

Dodgson, L. (2018). The 4 types of people narcissists

are attracted to, according to a psychotherapist. Retrieved from https://www.insider.com/the-types-of-people-narcissists-are-attracted-to-2018-8

Dodgson, L. (2018). Empaths and narcissists make a 'toxic' partnership -- here's why they're attracted to each other. Retrieved from https://www.businessinsider.com.au/why-empaths-and-narcissists-are-attracted-to-each-other-2018-1?r=US&IR=T

Evans, M. (2018). Retrieved from https://blog.melanietoniaevans.com/idolise-devalue-discard-the-3-phases-of-narcissistic-abuse-part-1/

Greenberg, E. (2017). How Does a Child Become a Narcissist?. Retrieved from https://www.psychologytoday.com/au/blog/understanding-narcissism/201705/how-does-child-become-narcissist

Grey, S. (2019). The Three Phases of A Narcissistic Relationship Cycle: Over-Evaluation, Devaluation, Discard - Esteemology. Retrieved from https://esteemology.com/the-three-phases-of-a-narcissistic-relationship-cycle-over-evaluation-devaluation-discard/

Grey, S. (2019). The Three Phases of A Narcissistic Relationship Cycle: Over-Evaluation, Devaluation, Discard - Esteemology. Retrieved from https://esteemology.com/the-three-phases-of-a-narcissistic-relationship-cycle-over-evaluation-devaluation-discard/

Lancer, D. (2018). Recovery from Codependency. Retrieved from https://psychcentral.com/lib/recovery-from-codependency/

Martin, S. (2018). How to Start Healing from Codependency. Retrieved from https://blogs.psychcentral.com/imperfect/2017/10/how-to-start-healing-from-codependency/

Narcissistic personality disorder - Symptoms and causes. (2017). Retrieved from https://www.mayoclinic.org/diseases-conditions/narcissistic-personality-disorder/symptoms-causes/syc-20366662

Quintana, S. (2019). The 7 Things You Must Do While Healing After Narcissistic Abuse. Retrieved from https://psiloveyou.xyz/the-7-things-you-must-do-while-healing-after-narcissistic-abuse-2901407efb54

Quintana, S. (2019). The 7 Things You Must Do While Healing After Narcissistic Abuse. Retrieved from https://psiloveyou.xyz/the-7-things-you-must-do-while-healing-after-narcissistic-abuse-2901407efb54

Setting Healthy Boundaries With The Narcissist In Your Life. (2018). Retrieved from https://www.

avalonmalibu.com/blog/how-to-set-healthy-boundaries-with-the-narcissist-in-your-life/

Shultz, D. (2019). On Narcissism and Healing from Narcissistic Abuse. Retrieved from https://medium.com/@dlshultz/on-narcissism-and-healing-from-narcissistic-abuse-9d10eea3f0a4

Tartakovsky, M. (2018). 10 Way to Build and Preserve Better Boundaries. Retrieved from https://psychcentral.com/lib/10-way-to-build-and-preserve-better-boundaries/

Utti, C. (2016). How to Fix an Addicted and Codependent Relationship | Willingway. Retrieved from https://willingway.com/fix-addicted-codependent-marriage/